Asylum Voices

Asylum Voices

Experiences of people seeking asylum in the United Kingdom

Editors
Dr Andrew Bradstock
Revd Arlington Trotman

Churches' Commission for Racial Justice

CHURCHES TOGETHER
IN BRITAIN AND IRELAND

Churches Together in Britain and Ireland
Inter-Church House
35–41 Lower Marsh
London SE1 7SA
Tel: +44 (0)20 7523 2121; Fax: +44 (0)20 7928 0010
info@ctbi.org.uk or (team)@ctbi.org.uk
www.ctbi.org.uk

ISBN 0 85169 287 7

Published 2003 by Churches Together in Britain and Ireland

Produced by Church House Publishing

Further copies available from CTBI Publications,
31 Great Smith Street, London SW1P 3BN
Tel: +44 (0)20 7898 1300; Fax: +44 (0)20 7898 1305;
orders@ctbi.org.uk www.chbookshop.co.uk

Cover designed by Church House Publishing
Cover photograph by Isabelle Merminod
Printed by Creative Print and Design Group, Ebbw Vale, Wales

Contents

Foreword

Asylum and immigration have become the major domestic issue we face in the United Kingdom today. Everyone from newspaper editors to television political commentators has an opinion on people seeking asylum. But while we are forever talking *about* them, we do not hear their voices. Just as the report *Faith in the City* (Church House Publishing, 1985) challenged society to hear the voices of those living in poverty and deprivation, so the need to hear people seeking asylum in Britain today can no longer be ignored.

This book attempts to put that right. It makes no claim to be an exhaustive analysis of asylum issues or the result of a long policy-forming process among the Churches. But whilst it may prompt such work, it seeks immediately to address the impact of the kind of attitude that was vividly portrayed in an anonymous letter I received following my call for justice and compassion for asylum applicants, as Moderator of the Churches' Commission for Racial Justice (CCRJ), on a BBC Radio 4 Sunday programme: 'Asylum seekers in the UK are confidence tricksters. They make up stories, they commit serious crimes and they support false religion. They increase house prices. If a white CofE USA person can be deported, so can all foreigners be deported.'

The authentic voice heard in this report is to make sure that in all future debate, the views of people seeking asylum and refugees themselves cannot be ignored. Along the way, it seeks to nail some misconceptions. It shows the arduous route and high personal costs involved in seeking asylum; no one does something that difficult without compelling reason. It further encourages us to engage with the human dimension of the issue, to see applicants as human beings created in the image of God, not as statistics.

In my episcopal ministry I found that many church congregations in both rural and urban areas wanted to be better informed, and surprisingly were much more generous in their judgements on people seeking asylum than sections of the press would have us believe. This report acknowledges that action on behalf of those in need is an essential part of a living faith in Christ (James 2.14-17), and many churches continue to offer support appreciated by asylum claimants. Loving your neighbour as yourself and working for justice is at the heart of what it means to be a real Christian. *Asylum Voices* will provide the opportunity for Christians and other faith groups to continue to prioritize prayer for those seeking asylum, and for Government to reassess policy.

Go before us, Lord Christ,
with the blessings of your goodness
and guide all those you call to authority
in the way of justice,
the knowledge of your liberty
and the wisdom of your gentleness;
for your Name's sake. Amen.

(*Celebrating Common Prayer*)

The Rt Revd Roger Sainsbury, Moderator of CCRJ
London, 2003

Acknowledgements

It would not have been possible to produce this report without the skill, foresight and energy that was invested in the task of listening. It was essential to place at the heart of it a process that would enable people seeking asylum in the United Kingdom themselves to share their stories in an atmosphere of freedom and trust. We are deeply indebted, therefore, to all those who made possible the interviews which constitute the core research, and particular gratitude is owed to refugees and people seeking asylum who agreed to talk about their experiences.

We are especially grateful to Jennifer Monahan, assisted by Caroline Howard and Katharine Fletcher, for undertaking the awesome and complex task of conducting the research. Grateful thanks are also due to all those who have provided advice and offered critical insights on the issues, including many non-governmental organizations (NGOs) working with those seeking asylum, not least the Medical Foundation for the Care of Victims of Torture, legal advisors, doctors, visitors to detainees, volunteers, caseworkers and other support groups.

This report could not have progressed to publication without the understanding and support of CTBI's Publications Committee, and the co-operation of the staff at Church House Publishing. We gratefully acknowledge the crucial interventions and support from the CCRJ Executive Committee who offered analysis and advice on substantive issues and process, which at times became difficult and painful. We commend Bev Thomas for her assistance to the committee in reading and preparing portions of the texts and addressing other aspects of the administrative process.

Finally, grateful thanks to all those from whom we needed to secure permission for use of copyright materials, including the Refugee Council and the British Medical Association. If we have overlooked anyone we sincerely apologize and would seek to make appropriate amends.

Introduction

As migration flows increase around the world, the need to protect and support displaced persons not only increases, but also becomes a human rights concern. People seeking asylum in the Western world are often vilified and demonized, and have been especially marginalized in the British context. It is entirely outrageous that some have been killed as a result. The Churches' concern with the plight of seekers today is rooted in the belief that all people share a common humanity and should, therefore, be treated justly.

Asylum Voices seeks to demonstrate that, far from being a faceless category to be shunned, those seeking asylum are people with deeply disturbing stories that demonstrate a truth often unheard or unrecognized in what has become an unfortunate political drama. It is the chief reason why, and perhaps how, Government and the people are encouraged to listen to, and reaffirm, the dignity and intrinsic human value of asylum applicants.

We are called to recognize the scriptural injunction not to oppress strangers and indeed to welcome them; for God desires that justice should prevail in our communities so that all might live according to the principles of equality and freedom. The Churches' Commission for Racial Justice (CCRJ), a commission of Churches Together in Britain and Ireland (CTBI), commissioned *Asylum Voices* in order to hear from seekers' own lips. We logged 146 interviews with persons from 37 countries between February and December 2001. (References to policy issues in the report have been updated to reflect the Nationality, Immigration and Asylum Act 2002.)

Table 1: Interviewees by country, number and percentage

Country	No. of interviewees	% of total
Afghanistan	13	9
Algeria	9	6
Czech Republic	7	5
Democratic Republic of Congo	7	5
Iran	18	12
Iraq	24	17
Sri Lanka	6	4
Zimbabwe	6	4
Others	56	38
Total	146	100

Gender:
Females 38   Males 108

Table 2: Age of interviewees by number and percentage

Age group	No. of interviewees	%
Under 20	10	7
20–30	72	49
30–40	47	32
Over 40	17	12
Total	146	100

Table 3: Status of interviewees when interviewed

Length of time in UK	No final result on asylum claim	With final result (ILR or ELR)[1]
0–6 months	36	–
6–18 months	29	10
18 months–3 years	21	6
3–6 years	11	6
Over 6 years	2	12

Note: These figures do not amount to the total interviewed because some interviewees, the wives, had not made asylum claims of their own, but depended on their husbands' claims.

As Table 3 shows, almost 75 per cent of those interviewed were still awaiting the final outcome of their asylum claims.

Asylum Voices also attempts to show that the popular dismissal of those seeking asylum as 'bogus', 'scroungers', 'aliens', 'potential terrorists' fundamentally denies their humanity and is often politically misleading. Read it, and you will see that only one label is really appropriate: fellow human beings, to whom all respect and support is owed, and who are gifted and skilled in many areas.

Immigrants and refugees have historically enriched and enhanced the cultural, religious, economic and political life of British society. They should not be treated with hostility and suspicion. Just and informed action is required (i) if people seeking an escape from abject – often Western-imposed – poverty are not to be denied asylum, and (ii) if the public is to be informed of the facts. Whilst we recognize the constant threat of evil in contemporary society, it is unjust to treat all people seeking asylum as 'terrorists'.

Asylum Voices acknowledges that immigration and asylum policies are increasingly primarily debated and planned at European level, but emphasizes the importance the Treaty of Amsterdam (1999) places on the matter. It asserts 'absolute respect for the right to seek asylum' based on the 'full and inclusive application of the 1951 Geneva Convention and its 1967 Protocol'.

This report seeks to illustrate why claimants left their countries and chose Britain as a place of refuge, and how current procedures and practices affect them, particularly highlighting their experiences of detention in the British judicial system. It considers how and what kind of support people seeking asylum get, and offers some theological reflection on the issues, whilst illustrating the difficulties around integration. The socio-economic and spiritual importance of work for many is combined with insights on the invaluable resource refugees represent. Crucially, this report tells of the extent to which asylum claimants' health worsens after reaching Britain, and notes some insights about their expectations for the future. It concludes with critical indicators for improvement in policy and practice and where hope may lie.

We hope that Church leaders, congregations and the general public will use this report to inform and stimulate debate and understanding, while frankly and robustly discussing the issues.

To leave one's home, family and familiar surroundings has always been a challenge, and it is made significantly harder when expectations are unrealized. People have migrated for centuries, but to be forced to flee one's land in haste and in search of safety, and then to be confronted with hostility and denial, raise important questions about leaving.

CHAPTER ONE

Why did you leave?

'No one would like to leave their lifelong friends.' (*Female, 17, Afghanistan*)

'Hear my prayer, O Lord, and give ear to my cry; do not hold your peace at my tears. For I am your passing guest, an alien, like all my forebears.' (Psalm 39.12)

The impression some politicians and sections of the media give is that people who arrive in Britain seeking asylum are simply out to find the country that is the 'softest touch'. Having endured a low standard of living in their own countries, they are lured to Britain by stories of a benefit system that enables people to live in comfort without having to work. Pejorative terms such as 'scrounger' and 'bogus' are used indiscriminately to popularize this myth, yet the reality could not be more different.

Choice or fear?

If there is one message that emerges from our conversations with people seeking asylum, it is that they did not leave their homes, family and friends by choice. Their decisions were not calculated or even rational: indeed, they could seldom even be called decisions, more reactions to factors beyond their control. Far from enjoying the luxury of choosing at leisure a country to which to emigrate, asylum claimants spoke of having no option but to leave. Sometimes they left hurriedly and in panic, sometimes after a slower accumulation of repression, injustice and deprivation. Almost invariably, what drove them to leave was fear – fear for their lives, for their safety, for their future, for their children's future, fear that life would be cut short, blighted, wasted.

In this work, we hear from some of the 22 million refugees[1] whom the United Nations High Commissioner for Refugees (UNHCR) considers 'of concern', who get no further than a refugee camp in a country next to their own.[2] Many more never make it across the border and thus become 'internally displaced persons' (IDPs). Only a small proportion have the energy, ingenuity and stamina to make the journey from their own continent, and only a few can access the funds that can buy a passage to safety. All of this raises the question of identity.

What is a refugee?

It became clear from the stories told that the reasons people fled their countries actually fell within the original intention of the UN Refugee Convention. The United Nations Convention Relating to the Status of Refugees, drawn up in 1951, defined a refugee as someone who, 'owing to a well-founded fear of being persecuted for reasons of race, religion, nationality, membership of a particular social group or political opinion, is outside the country of his nationality and is unable or, owing to such fear, is unwilling to avail himself of the protection of that country ...'.[3] This definition was drafted in the aftermath of the Holocaust. It applied only to Europe, and seems to have envisaged a white, politically active man from a country on the other side of the Cold War split. The UN Convention was revived and strengthened 16 years later with the addition of a Protocol Relating to the State of Refugees, which, crucially, called on its signatories to apply the original Convention 'without any geographic limitation'. Interestingly, as the scope of the Convention has broadened geographically over the years, the way it has been interpreted has narrowed. Now it is seen less as a way of offering protection to people fleeing persecution than as providing a set of criteria for excluding them.

In practical terms, in the British context, there is also a different understanding of 'refugee' and 'asylum seeker'. A 'refugee' refers to an asylum seeker who has been granted status – Indefinite Leave to Remain (ILR) or, until November 2002, Exceptional Leave to Remain (ELR). ELR has now been replaced by a discretionary protection category. Regardless of the status of people fleeing to the UK, all are troubled and fearful.

From fear to fear

People seeking asylum told us that they find in their country of 'refuge' fresh reasons for fear, principally the fear of being deported. When their claims for asylum are refused – as the majority are – they feel even more insecure as they wait for an appeal hearing. This may be a year or more hence. Some British newspapers see no contradiction in dismissing people seeking asylum as 'bogus' on one page, while reporting the conflicts from which they have fled on another. Some government departments can also reflect this attitude. In one context seekers are victims, in another a threat. If reporting in all sections of the media is to be coherent, and our domestic and foreign policy is to be fact-based and synchronized, we are compelled to listen to the accounts of asylum applicants and refugees themselves.

The treatment of seekers from Zimbabwe tells a salutary story. Although numbering only a few hundred, they were a new category and, as such, treated with greater suspicion than normal. Every effort was made by the authorities to deter further seekers, and those already present had their claims categorized as likely to be unfounded and refused within a week. Many were held in our oldest and most unsuitable prisons and then deported. All were of African origin. The Home Office decision-makers appeared to choose to ignore the Foreign Office's concerns over the situation in Zimbabwe, and the domestic and foreign messages were not 'joined up'. It was not until an outcry among NGOs, sections of the media and in parliament, that deportations to Zimbabwe were suspended.

Governments in the West appear still to endorse the humanitarian principles of the Convention and its Protocol, but in practice tend to manip-ulate them to serve political, commercial and diplomatic priorities. The grounds the Convention sets out for granting asylum, however, remain valid, and still appear to mirror the reasons why people flee their homeland. The testimonies of those seeking asylum in the UK today suggest that 'fear' still reflects the reality, but often the words of seekers are not trusted, as in the case of some Zimbabweans.

Though the issues in Zimbabwe are complex, Zimbabweans, like those seeking asylum from other countries, told stories that reflected the letter and spirit of the Convention: they were politically active, under the fear of persecution, and afraid to return. Yet, they also differed from the Convention in two important aspects: their country's government had, until recently, been considered eligible to buy British arms; and they were black. It is a sobering thought that the asylum debate cannot helpfully proceed without the clear acknowledgement of the reality of racism, as research repeatedly shows.[4] Applicants seeking asylum from sub-Saharan Africa (excluding the Horn) almost always receive a routine refusal, and Zimbabweans were no exception.[5]

Ethnic and religious factors

The conflicts that impel most people to flee their homeland have an ethnic (racial) component.[6] In many cases people seeking asylum are members of different ethnic, tribal or religious groups facing persecution and threat of death, starvation and dispossession, social exclusion and in some cases extinction. The accounts we heard provide individual glimpses of shared suffering. They help to explain why Western governments avoid recognizing *groups* as refugees, fearing potential numbers, and why members of such groups often fail to understand the need to prove *individual* persecution, perceiving their plight as collective.

The Kurds are a classic example of a group that has been systematically persecuted, not only on ethnic grounds but also because of deep-seated opposition to their national aspirations. One Iraqi Kurd gave a graphic account of the use of chemical weapons against the Kurds of Halabja in 1988:

'I have been a refugee twice in my life. My hometown is Halabja and I still remember when Chemical Ali [the nickname of one of Saddam's generals] bombed us with chemicals. They say that 5,000 died that day, but believe me, it was more like 8,000. I lost a sister that day. First they used ordinary bombs and the reason they did that was so that people would go down into the basements to shelter. The reason they wanted us to stay in was that the gas was heavy and would sink so they could kill more people. I don't know why, but I stood up on our roof – it was flat. There were dead people every- where. There is a famous photograph of a man dead with his baby dead in his arms. That was a neighbour of ours. He had six daughters and then his wife gave birth to a boy, and he was walking down the street to show people when the attack started. We were lucky we had a car and when we realized what was happening we drove and drove. When we came back there were just people lying on the street. It was horrible, horrible. There was a smell of bananas from the gases.'

Two young Hutu men from Rwanda were barely into their teens when they witnessed the deaths of family members in the genocide of April–May 1994. One said that he escaped by luck: he was away from his home when the killers came.

'I just left Rwanda suddenly because my family was killed in 1994. Then [later] because I was studying in Uganda in a seminary they came and took us into the bush for training, because they wanted us to fight. They were Tutsi soldiers. We decided to run away, three of us. But unfortunately one of my friends died on the way. We left him there.'

The other boy managed to save his life by pretence: 'back home, we were all mixed up. We had to claim what we were not. I had to tell people that I was Hutu – after my brother and father went missing.'

The Rwandan experience has an obvious parallel in Europe with the Bosnian war and ethnic cleansing of the Kosovan Albanians. A Kosovan boy describes his experience of ethnic cleansing: he was 16 at the time.

'It's been bad since I was been born, but it was really bad later. In 1989, 1993, 1998. 1998, like, exploded. Everywhere. Much of it was not fighting, just Serbs killing people – kids, women, men. Kicking them out. You don't see any resistance, because it's all civilians.

There's no way you could fight unarmed with someone who's on drugs, crazy, wants blood. I was born in south-west Kosovo, where the situation got so bad everyone was trying to get away. I wanted to try the city, Pristina, to see if it was better. I could be dead in a second. I was forced to leave. I went on my own to Pristina. I was not long there. My family, I don't know where they are right now. I've tried to get in touch ...'

Fighting to preserve the cultural identity of one's people can be another reason for having to leave one's homeland. An indigenous Indian leader from Bolivia spoke of defending the centuries-old culture of his people from those who would take their land.

'... All that I was doing was defending my people ... I was fighting for my sense of cultural identity. To get back our history that had been castrated ... I analysed all these things and explained them to my people. They understood their rights and began to form a rebellion but it was suppressed ...'

A former landowner whose family have traditionally been at the head of one of the oldest Arab tribes in south-west Iran told us how he was driven from his region by the dominant (Persian) majority. His father and uncles had been killed, and their land expropriated – valuable natural resources, in this case oil, were again at stake. He himself trained and worked as a teacher.

'I was not allowed to teach Arabic to my own children. I had to teach Farsi ... If a teacher is caught teaching Arabic they deprive you of your job and transport you to a Farsi-speaking area, which will be a long way away. Any action that suggested Arab nationalism is punishable by death ...'

Neither of these men dwelt on the fact that they had been repeatedly tortured. Indeed, the Arab tribal leader did not mention it at all – we learnt it from his interpreter, who explained: 'he doesn't see why he should talk about his individual experience – so many have gone through it'.

An ethnic group with, as the Convention puts it, a 'well-founded fear of being persecuted', is the Roma (gypsies) of central and eastern Europe. Roma speak of living a ghetto-like experience and even of suffering apartheid. One Roma spoke of not wanting his Slovak wife, a white woman, to get into trouble by associating with him, and made a habit of walking separately from her in the street. A Czech Roma mentioned how, when his wife tried to flag down a taxi to take her small son to hospital, a taxi driver stopped but said he would take 'the white lady' with her instead.

It is customary to categorize the Roma's reasons for leaving their way of life as economic.[7] Unemployment is certainly a big issue, but the accounts we heard suggest that it is seldom the sole reason, and not necessarily the decisive one. It often takes something more threatening – typically a violent incident or attack – to make a Roma family leave their homeland. A Roma woman from Slovakia described the climate of fear in which her family lived, and attacks on two relatives:

'All time weekends, we won't go the beach, to the water; we couldn't go, because they not like us there. Every weekend in the night, we wait inside, because maybe they kill us. They push my uncle, he fell, broke his leg. My dad was going home from job in motorbike, he coming from work, people – not skinheads – attacked him, punched him to the floor. My dad fell off a bridge.'

In the accounts we heard from Roma, that fear of direct life-threatening violence was a recurring feature. Many showed us newspaper articles describing attacks on people they knew, some close relatives and lifelong friends. Some situations bore similarities to pogroms. Some refugees from eastern Europe looked back to the Communist era with something akin to nostalgia. Their view was that in those days the authorities managed to keep a lid on the hatred, but that free travel and free expression had now put paid to that.

Another reason why Roma leave is the feeling that their children have no future. The relegation of Roma children to 'special' schools, which are meant for those with mental health problems, ensures that they end up unqualified. A Czech Roma teenager who had just passed her GCSEs in England told us:

'When I was six years old I went to psychologist doctor for check up, to decide [if I should go to] special or normal school. He said, "What's the money [currency] in Germany, Holland?" I said, "I don't know." He said, "Gypsy, special school".'

Religious persecution

Ethnicity, tribe, class and gender appear to have been significant reasons for persecution, though sectarian religious persecution could account for the reign of the Taliban in Afghanistan. It was the main reason quoted by several Muslim asylum applicants who spoke to us; yet it was allied to politics and score-settling, as in the case of a Shi'a whose family had served the former power:

'Taliban had a list of people who were Shi'as. Also, [I left] because of previous activities. Two of my uncles were killed, my brother, my father, and my name [was] also on a list. Being a Shi'a Muslim is a crime in Afghanistan. Taliban declared that Afghanistan is not a country for Shi'as, so they have to go out. Villages were burnt, [anyone] who had some money just fled from Afghanistan.'

Education under the Taliban was not allowed. We met Afghan refugees who were teachers, doctors, engineers, airline pilots, journalists. One of the latter had been openly critical of the regime:

'The Taliban captured my province in September 2000. I was there. I had to escape. I wrote many articles against the Taliban before they come to the province. They don't like criticism. When they captured Kabul, I and my friend escaped. They were shooting at us. He was killed later by the Taliban. He was very intelligent – a commander. I have three children, a girl aged 7, a boy aged 5 and a girl aged 3. I don't know where they are, where my wife is. My parents, brothers, sisters, I have no information ...'

The situation in Algeria in the early 1990s bore some similarities to that in Afghanistan under the Taliban. A year after the Islamic Salvation Front came to victory at the polls a professional couple saw the writing on the wall and left. The husband explained:

'In Algeria, the danger was in the same stairwell. The man delivering death threats – he's the one you could have been having coffee with this morning, lunch with yesterday. The danger is everywhere, all around. I've never hidden my opinions. I was anti-fundamentalist. At that time (1993), 3,000 only had been killed – it's terrible to say "only" but it turned out to be just a start. One of my friends was killed. Then I received a threatening letter from the Islamists ... and ... another letter, then a third. I told only three people. Two days later, all the area knew about it. They spread a rumour – if he doesn't comply, his throat will be cut in two days.'

Religious persecution on its own was cited as a cause for leaving by only a handful of the claimants who talked to us. We met four men who had fled Iran because of their conversion to Christianity or to a related non-Islamic sect. In one case the man's family as well as the regime were hostile to his religion:

'I was away working in Korea, four years, and going to church every week. When I was back in Iran, I carry on to the church again. After

one year, the security forces in Iran arrested me ... They make a lot
of persecution in all my body. So much blood came out of my body.
At that time, I lost my consciousness. I don't know how I got to the
hospital ... My father, while taking dinner, says, "You don't want to
tell your family what happened?" I said, "I have no feeling at the
moment" (I couldn't walk). My father, he got very angry, he said,
"I know what happened, you go to church." All my family, they were
angry with me. My father said, "You are not my son. Get out of my
home!"'

We also met a seeker persecuted in China for his active membership of
Falun Gong, a spiritual sect that has mushroomed despite repression by the
authorities.

'[I was arrested because] I wrote an article ... in favour of Falun Gong.
[It said] ... people in China don't have any freedom ... The purpose
of my coming to UK is to reveal the dark side of China. I want to
use my articles to clear the feudal ideology in Chinese people's minds
... I was imprisoned for a year – beaten with metal rods, electrical
rods.'

Nationality

Persecution on grounds of nationality is also common. The breakup of the
Soviet empire has led not only to a complicated situation in the Caucasus,
but also to difficulties for people of certain nationalities. A professional
musician explained how she left the region because there were too many
'nationality problems':

'My husband is Georgian; my husband's mother is Ossetian.
Georgians were kicked out from Azbkhazia and their homes taken
over. You can't live in Georgia. After Chechnya, they [Russians] don't
ask you if you're Chechnyan or Georgian. We look Caucasian. They
can kill you [in Russia] just because you look like that ... Where can
we live? Now it's Russian territory ...'

By comparison, the nationality dilemma of the Palestinians is relatively
simple, and has political consequences. Few refugees could define their
situation in as few words as this:

'I am a Palestinian and I live in Lebanon. I have no right to work, no
medical care. I have no nationality. I lived a whole life in Lebanon,

still I didn't get a nationality. It's a political thing. If they give nationality to Muslims, the elections will turn against them.'

Political opinions and the military

Political activism continues to attract persecution from corrupt regimes, and can also be a cause for people fleeing their homes. A human rights activist from Cameroon argued that although the country was democratic on paper, in reality it is not possible to challenge the government:

'Before I joined the [opposition Social Democratic Front] I was a member of the Human Rights Defense Group. It was necessary because of many human rights abuses. Lots of abuses are still going on at present. The challenge put me in danger. I was detained in Cameroon five times ... The fact is, if you're detained on political grounds, they give you extra treatment ... As a common man, you have no voice. The last time I was held, I was taken out on bail – a Party member bailed me out. I was supposed to report to the court, but I left before that.'

A 30-year-old Sudanese man left his home after suffering because of his work for the Communist Party:

'At 17 I joined the Communist Party in Sudan. I was still at school. I was not active. The thing that got me into trouble was when I joined a demo for one of our number who was killed in prison, by torture. I organized a safe house for the main people in the demo. I was captured and held for two months. They tortured me. I signed some paper saying I renounced all political involvement. After that I have to sign at security police every day, and I had to give notice if I wanted to travel outside Khartoum. I lost everything – I couldn't go to university. I started working as a trader, did that for three years. Meantime I joined up with friends and we started collecting information about human rights in the war area (the south). I knew I was at risk if they catch me ...'

Unaffiliated political activism can also lead a person to migrate and seek asylum. This doctor from Russia claimed that his environmental campaigning put his life in danger, both under the former Communist regime and after the change of government. The Home Office in the UK recognized his claim to be a political refugee:

'The hospital where I worked was near a chemical plant. I realized some of my patients were having stillbirths, infertility, abnormalities.

I started to make research (in the 1980s), gathering information. I realized that all the environmental data they [the Party] published was faked. I spoke to some scientists – chemists. They said, "Of course they're faked!" They are checked by special services – KGB ... So – I lost my job. My idea was to direct my research in the right direction – without much shouting. Get the facts, bring it out to the West, and get the West to help us. But somebody was watching, the KGB ... It got worse. In the early nineties, I was beaten up, my car was stopped, my telephone was tapped. Industry equals money. Huge money ... The government in those countries [former USSR] *is* the Mafia, the Mafia *is* the government.'

Being a dissident in Nigeria at a particular time could also have led to serious trouble:

'[He] came to my area to buy men to stand in support of him, to vote for him ... I did not want to vote for him, so I talked with some of the men around me [and] they said, "It's not a good thing to go and vote for this man, he's a dictator." Because of this they sent men to arrest me. They took me to prison. There they tortured me. Some other people there died as a result of beating. I almost died ... friends ... got us [out] through the back door ... They made a fake passport and said I should be going out of the country, and made the arrangement. They were looking for me. They came to my house, they arrested my wife and my kids, two boys, seven and eight. They killed them.'

This man's claim for asylum in the UK was still unresolved after five years, which included a long spell in detention.

A common reason for fleeing is being caught on the wrong side of a conflict, or military personnel being on the wrong side on any particular day! Soldiers make a recognizable target. One man from the Democratic Republic of Congo, judged a rebel under its dictatorship, described the treatment he received during detention by government forces – water torture, electric shock, being kept in darkness, and so on. Another man, one of the soldiers who went on the run following the change of power which brought Laurent Kabila to power, described the manhunt carried out by Kabila's forces on Mobutu's men, including arbitrary arrest, imprisonment and torture. This man had been press-ganged into fighting for UNITA in neighbouring Angola, before finally fleeing from Africa and reaching Dover.

Women: a 'social group'?

Some forms of persecution can be specific to women. In many societies, a woman who has been raped suffers not only the original trauma but also the terror of the social and domestic consequences. A woman can be utterly devalued by a society if it is known she has been raped: as one rape victim from Sri Lanka told a doctor with the Medical Foundation for the Care of Victims of Torture, 'If it's known, the women will line up to spit at me and the men will line up to rape me.' Intimidation, including rape, is one of the oldest and most widespread methods of terrorizing not only women but whole families and entire communities.

The following account, from a woman of the Shansi clan in Somalia, is an example of how vulnerable women are in the context of ethnic and tribal warfare. She describes events during the civil war of 1991–3 and has clear grounds to claim, in the words of the 1951 Convention, a 'well-founded fear' of persecution as both a woman and a member of a minority ethnic grouping:[8]

> 'Ten days after the fighting started and things seemed to have calmed, my sister went to the market to try to get some food. The fighting worsened again whilst she was out and she did not return. We never heard anything about her – maybe if she had been killed her body would have been found. Perhaps she was actually kidnapped. At that time the government and the rebels kidnapped many women. They just did what they liked with them ... On the same day, ten Hawiye militias looted our house. They broke down the front door and came into the room. They started shouting insults at us, saying, "You Shansis, you are strangers, what are you doing in Somalia?" Then they grabbed my mother and me. When my father tried to stop them they shouted that he couldn't do anything to them and they shot him dead. When we saw what they had done to my father we ran over to him crying. They ordered us to stop and then started to beat me and my mother with their rifle butts. They hit my mother in the face until her teeth fell out. I was also beaten on the head and it was cut open. I still have scarring. The beating was so intense that I collapsed ... My mother told me that they searched the house, took everything that we had and then left ... The militias came to our house again because they knew we could not protect ourselves. We had no guns ...'

In 2000, Somalia gained a transitional government but still lacked a central judicial or police system. Somali refugees come mainly from the minority clans that have no militias to protect them and no political power base.

If the Convention Relating to the Status of Refugees were to be brought fully up to date, 'gender' would be added to the list of grounds for well-founded fear of persecution. Given that such an addition is unrealistic, with the Convention itself under threat, the only option available has been to tuck women under the wing of an existing category, the obvious one being 'a particular social group'. Ireland opted for this approach with its first domestic asylum law in the mid-1990s, and the Canadian Immigration and Refugee Board decided to 'see how the Convention could fit the experience of women'.[9] Most other jurisdictions are ignoring the experience of women, though decisions in the British courts on individual cases have provided groundbreaking exceptions. The most notable was the Shah and Islam ruling in 1997 (Imm. AR 145), in which the House of Lords accepted that women in Pakistan were a 'particular social group': removal to Pakistan was ruled out because of the likelihood of punishment by stoning.

Guidelines on gender provided by leading women lawyers, academics and the Immigration Appellate Authority are accepted by adjudicators in principle, if not always in practice. A woman can be doubly vulnerable: she may be targeted in her own right for any of the reasons that a man is, and also as a surrogate in her role as wife, mother, daughter or sister. The fundamental inequalities in wealth and power in many traditional cultures also put women at risk of violence in their own homes (honour killings being an extreme example), and this inequality can form a backdrop to other forms of violence. A Somali woman whose family was driven out by a dominant clan said as part of her answer to the question 'Why did you leave?':

'There is a lot of problem for women, begging money from men. They are suffering a lot at home. Men have always the upper hand: if he want he can kick her, he can do with women as he likes.'

The words 'vulnerable' and 'victim' are routinely attached to women asylum applicants. Vulnerable they certainly are, but victims many are not. Most of the women we talked to are survivors, and several were among the most courageous and determined of all the people we met. Once their own problems as refugees start to recede a striking number of women take on the problems of others. Two Sudanese women we spoke to are catalysts in organizations offering help to fellow Sudanese refugees: they have transferred their cause from there to here. One recounted her dreadful experience:

'I had been interrogated, kicked off my work, had verbal abuse. Being a single woman, I was so afraid that things will happen. We started to organize demonstrations asking for different things. Lots of people disappeared in "ghost houses", places where people were tortured to death. We organized as women. … We got normal women to demonstrate, they were targeting those who are really activist … They forced people in the workplace to dress in a certain way, also to stop everything and go to pray at prayer time. Each work place had a prayer room attached. They were *forcing* these things on people … Twice, three times a week I was interrogated … It was psychological pressure, nerve-breaking.'

These women were rare in maintaining the liberty of being single. A woman who is a wife and a mother automatically adds a 'gender' dimension to other categories under which she may be persecuted.

Victims of sexual abuse, of both sexes, do not talk about their experiences, particularly not to a stranger. Until the last fortnight of our period of interviewing, no one, man or woman, had described or even mentioned rape as a reason for fleeing, even though we knew from intermediaries that that was what some had suffered. In the penultimate week of our interviews, however, one young woman who had just come out of detention in the UK was asked by the prison visitor who had befriended her if she would agree to give an interview. She was from Uganda. When asked what happened to make her leave she said:

'Just before the elections … they came and attacked us at home. They said, "You remember what happened to your family – your father was killed, your mother was hurt [she had seen her raped]. Now, you continue to support the wrong party." They were beating us. They tied us up naked outside. The children were there, two twin boys, they were aged four. They had to [be left to] cry and cry. We couldn't move. We were put in a vehicle and went a long distance … they took us to a very big house – like a warehouse, but inside were small rooms, very small rooms. They carried me out. In these rooms, you could stand or squat – you couldn't lie down. I was kept naked for the whole time. Almost two weeks I was there. I was raped. I don't know who [it was]. It was dark – I couldn't even see how many. There was a small bucket. "If you need to help [relieve] yourself – there's the bucket." Then he [the guard] give me something like a sheet to wrap around, to go to see an officer. Officer say, "Do you know why you are here?" "No." "You've been campaigning. You've been telling people about kidnapping and being taken to fight."'

Human beings in extraordinary situations

People seeking asylum are fellow human beings in extraordinary situations. With the services of a good lawyer they may prove to the authorities that they have a 'well-founded fear' of being persecuted in their own country and merit protection as a refugee. However, the reasons asylum applicants give for leaving are more likely to win them discretionary ELR or the stay on deportation allowed by the Human Rights Act. This prohibits a person being returned to a situation where they risk facing inhuman or degrading treatment – but even this is only granted where an appeal is successful, and it may well not be. Interpreted correctly for the protection of people seeking asylum today, the 1951 Convention would properly admit such cases. Though reasons given for claims often fall within broader categories than those listed in the Convention, a claimant's inability to meet the 'accepted criteria' does not make an asylum seeker 'bogus'.

A very common experience is that women seeking asylum are often dragged into cases involving men, whether or not they are directly impli- cated. Suspicion falls on the husband, the shadow falls on the wife. A Tamil woman in Sri Lanka put herself in danger, both as the wife of a human rights lawyer and as a trained lawyer herself, by helping with his workload:

> 'I left because of stresses and strains – there were searches in our houses, especially when I was expecting a child. My husband was arrested in 1990, '93, '94 – in spite of that, he continued, I was really with him, I handled cases. If someone comes and knocks, I go first and say – "Who are you?" I had to take risk by being his wife – we keep the phone out because we get so many threatening calls. Lots of risk with the children ...'

It was a particular incident in the street, in which she lost her unborn baby, that caused her and her husband finally to flee:

> 'We came here also because I underwent a great stress in February 1998. I was going to do a job for a client of ours at the police HQ, and I had a physical assault from a Sinhalese woman and I miscarried a baby. She stripped me. I was without clothes. She pressed on my stomach and I miscarried. We thought we would have a girl. It was our dream.'

Asylum applicants from Sri Lanka and Colombia related to us similar stories of being caught on the wrong side in situations of conflict. Before a ceasefire in 2002, the Tamil minority in Sri Lanka had for generations been sandwiched between two dangers: the insurgent Tamil guerrillas and the Sinhalese army. One Tamil interviewee had been arrested and had his house burnt down because his fishing boat had been used by the LTTE (Tamil Tigers). In Colombia, where a truce did not hold, one left-wing interviewee was threatened with death from paramilitaries because he had assisted guerrillas.

Another interviewee, who described himself as 'conservative', saw his son shot by hit men and was himself threatened. He told us: 'It's difficult in Colombia to know who's after you. I was called every day on the telephone, threatened. After one week, I decided to leave.'

The motive: seeking safety or economic migration?

Immigration authorities make a clear-cut distinction between 'genuine refugee' and 'economic migrant'. In practice, however, as often as not, political insecurity and poverty are inextricably linked in people's lives. Many see an asylum claim as an unavoidable expedient to ensure both safety and an income, as an Algerian made clear:

'Some people used to come here to work for four or five years and go back. [But] since 1990, people come here for survival. You don't get safe in Algeria, [and also] you can't get a house and you can't get married.'

As recent research[10] clearly shows, throughout history people have migrated, and modern Britain has been built with political, cultural, religious and social input from immigrants. Inevitably there will be migrants whose purpose is simply economic, though not surprisingly, few in this category were keen to talk to us. One man, from Fujian Province in southern China, disarmingly announced that, as a Christian, he would not tell a lie and therefore must make clear from the outset that his motivation for leaving China was economic. He seemed to equate applying for asylum with applying for a work permit. Back home all his efforts to make economic progress had failed. Falling foul of the official one-child policy had not helped. Here, he was living a life of unremitting servitude in the restaurants of Chinatown but was pleased to earn money. He had already paid off the 'Snakeheads' (Chinese smugglers) who had fixed his passage, which made him an exception.

Another man, also from China, had been less fortunate in finding continuous work in London. He described the situation that had driven him here, and again the Chinese prohibition on having a second child had played a significant role:

'I was jobless. I did manual labour, temporary work. I lived with my family – my parents, my wife, my daughter and son. We were under pressure from the [local] government. For different reasons. It is very hard to earn money. You were punished, had to pay huge fines. You were asked to pay local officials. For example, the one-baby policy. You have to pay a lot of money for two. Family planning has complicated regulations. Up to [the age of] 24 you are not allowed to have children. I was not younger, but my wife became pregnant for the second time. We rely on male labour in the country. If you have a girl, you want to have a boy. The second baby, that was my problem. Women have to go through a check to see they are not pregnant. If they find out your wife is pregnant, you're fined. No exact figure is announced. So the decision is reached by the local official, so if you don't get on with him, he asks more. If you pay without a receipt and at their home, you pay less. But if you go to the office and you get a receipt, then you pay more. I paid at the official's home. It was several thousand yuan. You must work more than a year to earn this money. I don't know how it is all over the country, but in my area, that's how it is. Many people try to escape.'

CHAPTER TWO

Why the United Kingdom?

'People pay up to five grand, ten grand for a family to get here. Why would they come for £28 a week?' (*Kosovan Albanian*)

'I was a stranger and you welcomed me.' (Matthew 25.35)

The first, and perhaps the most significant, response to the question 'Why Britain as the destination?' is simply that people seeking asylum do not choose Britain themselves. 'Agents', where these are involved, normally make the choice of destination and organize the journey for those who have no option but to rely on them.

Dependence or choice?

The reasons why people seeking asylum have used the Red Cross hangar outside Calais have more to do with dependence than with choice. Those seeking safety cannot leave their own countries legally because they do not normally possess passports (the issuing authority may well be the very government whose persecution they are trying to escape). They cannot exercise their right to claim asylum or seek employment legitimately – except in very restrictive circumstances – in an industrialized country. Visa restrictions and carrier liability (under the 1999 Immigration and Asylum Act, authorities could impound aircraft, ships and lorries and impose large fines on owners if they were discovered carrying people seeking asylum without papers) ensure that they have no legal access to the countries concerned. Those fleeing, therefore, have to put their lives in the hands of the agents or 'smugglers'.[1]

For substantial sums of money agents organize a way of getting people seeking asylum out of their own countries and into a Western state that, on paper at least, observes the 1951 Geneva Convention. From the moment they approach an agent they have little or no control over their destiny. A Tamil community leader who has worked in London for many years summed up the situation without hesitation: 'The asylum seekers don't decide. The agents choose which country they will come to.'

Each network of agents has its own points of contact, dictating where and how its human cargo will be transported. 'Agents have got their routes,' a young Kosovan explained, 'some to America, some to France, some to Britain. Everything is organized – they wait for you there …' Some claim that the drivers of the lorries transporting them knew they were among their cargo, while others mention being warned by agents not to make any sound while in transit in case they were discovered by the driver.

Transit routes are adjusted if necessary – for example, a civil war or other serious event may block a route through a country or region – but they do not disappear. The Calais–Dover crossing is a classic example of adjustment. A clamp-down on the Channel ferries shifted the 'clandestine' traffic to the Tunnel; stepped-up controls on the passenger trains put even heavier traffic on to lorries; radar checks on lorries led to even more desperate moves by individuals and families to jump freight trains; and beyond that, stories filtered out of families clinging to the underside of Eurostar trains and of people attempting to *walk* through the Tunnel. With the tightening of security at Calais some agents only assumed responsibility for getting their desperate human cargo as far as Calais, leaving them to negotiate the final – and hardest – part of the journey themselves, or with the help of another agent who would charge a high fee for reaching Britain.

Images of Britain

This does not explain, however, why people risk their lives trying to get to Britain from France, with or without the help of an agent. Sangatte Red Cross Centre has now closed, but the accounts we heard seem to suggest that the sales pitch of the agents reinforces a predisposition towards Britain already held by their clients. This is based on a widespread belief that Britain is a country that respects freedom, democracy and human rights, a picture painted by the media in the seeker's country of origin and by word of mouth. Use of the English language is also a strong attraction, and there is a feeling, sometimes based on first-hand experience, that other western European countries are less free and more racist.

So we found among interviewees an overriding expectation and hope that they would find in Britain the 'mirror opposite' of the situation that had led to their leaving their homeland. Personal safety came top of the list and was the single motive most often mentioned.

Below are some typical responses to the question 'What did you expect of the United Kingdom?' 'Safety' (*Roma man from the Czech Republic*). 'To feel secure' (*Sudanese woman*). 'I was expecting safety, life' (*Algerian man*). 'I had a good life there, but I wasn't safe there. Only I came here to be safe' (*Iranian man*).

'Safety' was the answer that came back repeatedly. It is also what those in search of asylum want to hear – and do hear – from agents. Those in danger and leaving in haste have no autonomy or choice. This, too, was spelt out time and again:

'The agent told me we were going somewhere safe. I didn't know where. He told me when I go there I'd be helped and if I come here people would help me find my relatives ...' (*Young man from Rwanda*)

'The agent took me to Britain, somewhere to be safe. Britain is a safe country. First of all my life is safe.' (*Young Afghan man*)

Hearsay in countries of origin, or in transit countries, lays a fertile base for the agent's reassuring version of life in Britain. Again, the accounts we heard were strikingly similar, and upbeat:

'I had heard many good things about the UK – that the government is generous, receptive to persecuted people.' (*Afghan student*)

'I had no contact with anyone in the UK but I got information about asylum seekers in newspapers in Iran. These were saying that refugees would get full refugee status, and that many were being deported from Italy, Turkey. I also heard about it from other people who worked in Iran who worked for the WCPI [Communist Party in northern Iraq] and who lived there ... I wasn't planning to come to a European country when I left Iraq, I was just hoping to come somewhere safer. I knew about the [1951] Convention and on that basis I thought that if [the UK] followed it, every refugee would get his right.' (*Iraqi Kurd*)

'I knew where I was going. The agent told me I was going to London. We agreed to London ... I thought it was going to be a nice place, I could get peace. I heard many people got peace. The agency told me it was a peaceful country ...' (*Young Somali*)

An imprecise vision of 'Europe' as a safe destination was expressed by a handful of interviewees, but again, the choice of the precise country rested with the people in whom they invested their money:

'The life I had in Afghanistan was like an animal. The agent told us he would take us to Europe and that we would be safe there. He said, "They will look after you, you will feel human." The agent had told us so many good things about living here. He said it would definitely be better for my son in particular. But he gave no details, just that life is good here.' (*Afghan man with 16-year-old son*)

'When I left Iraq I expect to go to a country no wars, no kill, no bloody. Europe, I think it is my choice. I can't explain everything, just I say I wanted to save my life and come to Europe. If I hadn't problems in my country I didn't leave my family. I miss them now ... I didn't know I was coming to British. When the police catch us inside the lorry they speak English and I asked them, "Is this British or not?" He said, "Yes, you speak English or not?" I say, "Yes, just a little."' (*Iraqi Kurd*)

Women tend to have even less input than men when it comes to arrangements for fleeing. A male relative is likely to be the person paying. One Kosovan woman left her country in a lorry with her young sons. She told us, 'It was my father-in-law's decision.' She had no idea where the lorry was going. 'When I left, I haven't think nothing. I just say, "I am in your hands, God."'

An African girl's account of her departure illustrates how the problems become compounded when a woman is also young. She explained why she wouldn't even dream of asking a senior relative for information:

'All my uncle gave me was a boarding card and a ticket. I don't know what he arranged [or] if he knew people at the airport. In Sierra Leone, people are not cheeky to their parents: they'd slap you if you were so, so I can't question him. He seemed really panicky. Maybe someone threatened him.'

English being a global language is also a key factor in determining why many seeking asylum head for the UK. Often, of course, the people who have been most exposed to Britain for education or employment purposes are likely to have studied English, but this was not generally understood as a benefit:

'I speak English well. First reason [for not going elsewhere], I would have had to learn a new language.' (*Iraqi Kurd*)

'I could speak the language. I preferred to go somewhere I could communicate.' (*Iraqi Kurd, university student*)

Benefits and freedom to work

None of the asylum interviewees we talked to said that they came to Britain in order to find work – although all assumed they would work having arrived. A minority said they expected some sort of subsistence at first, though treated with contempt the suggestion that they had come specifically in search of benefits:

'There's a lot of facts English people don't know ... People pay up to five grand, ten grand for a family to get here. Why would they come for £28 a week?' (*Kosovan Albanian*)

'I'm not interested in benefits. I have worked all my life. I didn't know about them before I came.' (*Iraqi Kurd*)

'We are coming here because we have had political problems, not for the money ... Each person coming here pays $5–6000 [to agents]. This is enough to live on sitting at home without work for five to ten years.' (*Young Kurds*)

After safety, the goal most often mentioned by our interviewees was 'freedom', including the freedom to earn a living. A number of people we talked to felt strongly that this was a natural and valid component of their concept of freedom. Freedom to work and earn and achieve independence comes in the same breath as political and religious freedom. One young Iranian man equated freedom to practise the religion of his choice with freedom to find a job: 'I like to be free,' he said, 'nobody bother me, have my own religion – because in Iran I couldn't change religion – and to find a job.' He then articulated a view often expressed by young asylum applicants:

'I had expected to go to college immediately to improve my knowledge. If I go to college I can find English; if I find English I can find a job and I can find my freedom.'

CHAPTER THREE

Procedures and process

'You cannot answer questions they do not put.' (*Zimbabwean man*)

'Truly I tell you, just as you did it to one of the least of these who are members of my family, you did it to me.' (Matthew 25.40)

To many observers, the asylum process in Britain is unnecessarily adversarial: instead of treating individual cases on their merits and taking a detached and impartial view of each applicant's claim, it places the onus of proof on the seeker.[1] In theory, the proof required is simple and general; in practice, what is demanded is very specific documentary evidence relating to the person's own individual situation. To make matters worse, before the seeker even has access to legal advice, it is not made clear to him or her what exactly has to be proved, or by what means.

Most of the people we interviewed had no idea what was involved in seeking asylum. Some were not even aware that asylum existed, or, if they were aware, that they might be eligible to apply for it. A Zimbabwean who insisted he had been detained and beaten up by government forces in his country told us that he thought asylum was only for people fleeing from civil wars like that in Bosnia. A Sudanese man who had been tortured went to Newcastle on arrival to avoid possible spies from his country's government in London. 'I [hadn't] any idea about asylum,' he told us, 'I didn't know I [had] a right. In Newcastle they advised me. I asked "What is asylum seeker?" They explained.'

Most people we met knew something of asylum from their agent, but had no idea of its procedures. The first hurdle was to discover how and where to lodge a claim.

Arrival

The start of the process for many asylum hopefuls involves being dropped by an agent, waiting in an airport or ferry terminal, and then finding their way to the immigration offices in Croydon. The first authorities they encounter are immigration officials and police, and we heard contrasting impressions of these officers. The police, particularly the Kent Constabulary, are widely found to be helpful. An Iranian man told us, 'When I arrived in the UK a policeman said to me: "Don't worry, I'll help you." He gave me a glass of coffee. I felt safe at that time. I didn't expect it.' A Kosovan Albanian who arrived at Dover described the police as very friendly:

'They gave us water, coffee – what you want. They were very nice people. I can't say other things, it's not true. They try to help but they can't break the law. Us don't know that law. When I came here I am illegal. Everywhere, English people help me.'

On the other hand, immigration officials appeared not to be such a reassuring presence. A Czech Roma told us:

'Immigration officer very crazy. No speak, quickly, quickly, he say "Go back [to Czech Rep]." Prison. Three and a half months in prison, Rochester ...'

An Afghan male had a similarly harrowing experience:

'[When I arrived at Dover there was] nothing at all. Just what's your name, where you from? They opened the door, said, "Go wherever you want." I said, "Send me somewhere"; they said, "No, it's your choice, go wherever." I asked, "Which charity is going to help me?" They said, "Migrant Helpline." They said, "Go wherever." I had no money, no English. You don't know where you are. They said, "Just go." People pointed me the way [to Migrant Helpline]. They gave me some money for food, send me to hotel.'

Some immigration officers were described as 'wicked' by a 21-year-old Nigerian male. He told us:

'I know they do their job. I met about three immigration officers – it was a bad experience. A lady came to ask me questions, "You are to tell us why you are here." "Because I want to seek asylum." They said I should not dream to see anything else, the detention centre was Britain for me. [They were] laughing at me, mocking me. I expected harsh speaking. I didn't expect mocking.'

'I want to know why you are coming here and asking for asylum,' a Sri Lankan Sinhalese woman with a 12-year-old daughter was asked at Heathrow. 'They didn't give me any advice about the law and they didn't offer me a lawyer. Then they gave me some forms and told me to fill it in. It said something about Human Rights – I don't know what. We were waiting for 11 hours.'

The interview

The substantive interview is the key element in the asylum process. Everything the asylum hopeful says and does not say will inform the whole course of the claim. Above all, evidence from the interview will be used to question the credibility of the claimant at the appeal.

Applicants are entitled to a Statement of Evidence Form (SEF) to take away and complete before being called to the main interview. Sometimes this does not happen. If arrangements can be made to conduct a substantive interview at the port of arrival, it goes ahead there. Immigration officers have to ascertain whether the applicant feels well enough to do the interview (in case its validity is queried later), but some of the people we met, who found themselves faced with this interview shortly after arrival, felt under pressure to do it immediately.

Other asylum applicants who underwent a full interview after a long journey spoke of waiting around all day at the port or airport, while others had slept rough on the airport concourse. They are patently not at their best when they first arrive in this country. 'When I came to England, it was holiday night', an Iranian man in Glasgow told us:

'Immigration Department said "At the moment everything is closed [it was New Year's Eve]. We fix up date tomorrow, arrange everything – interpreter, interview." I sleep in [the] airport. The interview was conducted the next day, 1 January, and lasted five hours. I was tired and a little bit hungry. The interview is very important, is my life. They asked me "Are you OK?" I was hungry and tired, but that is not important, and I wanted as soon as possible to depart from the airport. It was very noisy, lots of passengers.'

Clearly his concern to get away from the airport as soon as possible led him to agree to do the interview on the spot.

A Bolivian indigenous leader told us about his experience at Heathrow:

'When I arrived I was in a state that wasn't normal for me. My first problem was at the airport with the language. Then there was the interrogation. It is difficult to remember what was happening to me because of the psychological effects of what had happened to me ... I was really frightened that the information I was giving them would be passed on to the Bolivian authorities. It was like another interrogation. Remembering [what had happened to me] was really bad for me. It was another psychological trauma. The pressure of these questions – it was as if I wasn't in London. It seems like I was back in Bolivia. The only difference was that they weren't beating me up

... [The Home Office] didn't treat me like a leader but like a subversive. They asked me "How were you tortured?" This was very difficult to remember because I didn't want to remember.'

Many asylum applicants we spoke to considered that their interview had been designed less to assess the truth of their story than to outwit and trip them up. The Iranian we met in Glasgow compared his interview to a football game. 'She [the interviewing officer] wants to win, and I want to win, and she tries to trick me, so I have to show I'm good. [We were] kicking the ball back and here, back and here.'

Many saw the interview as a test, and wondered about the relevance of some of the questions they were asked. An Afghan man we talked to in Glasgow said that his interview seemed to be about establishing that he really did come from the country he claimed he did rather than about the issues that had led him to seek asylum:

'When I go for interview, they ask geography questions, don't bother to ask about your problems ... "Where is Thorncliffe Hotel? [a hostel near Heathrow where asylum seekers are housed for a few days on arrival]. How many houses in your village?" To find out where you're really from ... they say "Describe your flag", and "Name three previous governments". "What is the river in Afghanistan? What is the highest mountain? What is the radio [station] called?"'

Applicants who experienced this kind of interview felt they did not get a fair opportunity to put their case. As one Zimbabwean man put it, 'You cannot answer questions they do not put.' However, a small minority said they were happy with their interview and felt they had been given a fair chance to explain their case.

Several people we met let their story unfold in a way that would not have been possible under the 'straitjacket' routine of the immigration interview. We felt that some, had they told the immigration officer what they told us, would have risked making themselves hostages to fortune. One man we met in East London told us how the terrible reality of what had happened in his case – his mother and father had been killed and his sister raped in front of him – took a long time to surface. Early in the interview he had been preoccupied with a fear of not being allowed to work, and had told the Home Office that he did intend to work. This alone could have been taken, negatively, as an 'admission' that he was an 'economic migrant'.

Interviews may be particularly difficult for women, especially if they need to reveal details of sexual abuse to a male officer or through a male interpreter. The guidelines specify that women should question women with the help of women interpreters, but they are not always followed. 'Agnes' told us that she was taken off to a detention centre without her story of multiple rape being heard.

For some the initial processing is very demeaning. It is their first experience of not being believed, and the point where individual identity gives way to bureaucratic formulae. A Sudanese woman summed it up thus:

> 'It is a most inhumane thing, the officer who start questioning you will start not believing you, [there is an] air of suspiciousness. [They] ask you to make photo, stick it to paper. Your whole being will be minimized to that paper. You give up your passport.'

We learned that inaccurate record keeping and the way in which personal notes become detached from applicants' files is a feature of the whole asylum process, and causes much distress. A number of interviewees and lawyers we spoke to referred to lost documents – including passports, union membership cards and exam certificates – and of frequent delays caused by lost files. Several of our interviewees had had protracted problems in getting their basic details recorded correctly. Again, there is a sense of being stripped of identity. One Iranian Kurd, issued with a document bearing the wrong name and date of birth, commented:

> 'Is not nice, not good – name and date of birth, it's all you've got.'

Legal advice

Immigration procedures are complicated and change repeatedly. Proper legal advice is essential from the start if a full and accurate account is to be presented. The completion of the Statement of Evidence Form alone, 19 pages in English, demands specialist assistance. If the form is not returned within 14 days, the applicant is automatically refused on 'non-compliance' grounds. Yet the appropriate legal expertise is in critically short supply, and barely existed outside London before dispersal was implemented. It is not going to be readily available overnight. Many claimants in dispersal areas therefore cannot find accessible legal help, and have great difficulty maintaining contact with a London lawyer, assuming they found one before being dispersed. One Iraqi Kurd who had been dispersed to Coventry told us:

> 'The first time I tried to get an appointment with solicitors in Coventry they told me that there was a waiting list. I couldn't get an appointment until two months after the deadline for my form. When I arrived, they gave me no ID … I've never had my refusal translated to me.'

The poor quality of the advice received was another much-repeated theme. A large number of interviewees were not at all happy with their legal advisers. Their experience was that the advisers were only doing it for the money: 'It's a business', one applicant said. Another, an Iraqi, had an even more jaundiced view as a result both of his own case, and of interpreting for other asylum applicants. 'A solicitor is a liar,' he told us: 'He just makes promises but he can't do what he says. He tries to find a pretext [to charge you], he needs the money.'

Many interviewees mentioned changing lawyers – some two or three times – because the first one was 'bad', 'useless' or 'did nothing'. Some asylum detainees have claimed that unscrupulous legal advisers have been able to gain access to them in prison and obtain their signature for the purposes of claiming legal aid, and that thereafter they have heard nothing from them.

Detainees are particularly vulnerable when poorly represented. One result is that a bail application is rarely lodged on their behalf. Volunteer visitors often comment on the fact that solicitors seem not to care whether a client remains locked up or not.

An Iraqi Kurd, a doctor who also acted as an interpreter, suggested that 'asylum seekers are not just victims of the Home Office [but] ... of the solicitors'. On the other hand, the minority who were pleased with their lawyers were *very* pleased, valuing their personal commitment as well as their professionalism. 'Nina, my lawyer, she shows she understands,' a young woman from Sierra Leone told us, 'but at the airport, the Home Office, they're just doing their job, there's no emotion. Nina shows she cares, but she can't be unprofessional. She's the only person who cares.'

Another woman, from Sudan, said that her lawyer 'really was good. He showed that I had a case. He did his work.' However, whether lawyers were thought good or bad, a lack of the means to travel to see them had prevented several interviewees from attending appointments.

The Home Office

The Home Office's claim that they have made progress by speeding up and increasing efficiency in the system can often be a mere political reaction. Systemic inefficiency in some parts of the Home Office can add further to the difficulties faced by asylum applicants. For example, although interviews are held in London, Liverpool and Leeds, claimants housed in the south are sometimes called north, and those in the north asked to travel south. Interviews are often missed because a dispersed seeker did not have the money to travel to an interview several hundred miles away.

An Iranian in Glasgow told us that he had been called to Croydon by the

Immigration and Nationality Department but that the letter had arrived too
late for him to get there. The date was changed, but the second time

'they invited my wife instead of me. She went there, they said,
"Excuse me, this is a big mistake." Third time they invited me, but
didn't send train ticket. I went to the Post Office for something else
[a parcel], when I went there, they said, "This is for you, but the
address is not correct." When I got that letter, I saw they invited my
wife and they sent ticket for her again. I used her ticket and went to
Croydon.'

This would appear to be neither an exaggeration nor exceptional. A Tamil
woman from Sri Lanka told us how the wrong papers were served with her
notice of refusal so that her solicitor could not send in for an appeal:

'All the documents were wrong. They said I came for a Tamil
conference, which is not true. All different points – factual, as well
as legal errors …'

We also heard of a Congolese man in Kent whose wife had a heart
condition. On the Saturday of her operation he had to leave for his Home
Office interview in Liverpool, and because he did not qualify to have his
travel costs paid he took out a crisis loan of £170 to pay for his ticket. In the
end he was so distressed about his wife that he could not go through with
the interview and it had to be rescheduled. He had both to pay back the crisis
loan *and* get another for the rescheduled interview!

Interpreters

Another source of difficulty for people seeking asylum is a shortage of
qualified interpreters. This is compounded when people with little or
no experience of interpreting, or sometimes even of the language concerned, fill the gap. We learned of one student, recruited by an agency
to interpret for an immigration interview with a Nepalese applicant, whose
Nepalese consisted of what she had learned on a stay during her gap year.
When she realized what was required of her she made it clear she was
not able or willing to interpret for a second interview. Nevertheless, agents
acting for the Immigration Service put her under considerable pressure to
continue.

A Chinese man who runs a language school was critical of the British
Government for using Malay or Singapore Chinese to interpret even though
the languages are quite different and the interpreters do not understand the
context for the interpreting they are doing. He gave the example of a
mainland Chinese asylum seeker who described how for '15 years, I climb

up the mountain and walk through fields'. This is the Mandarin Chinese way of naming the re-education through manual labour that many intellectuals and political dissidents suffered in China. The Malay interpreter, however, translated that as 'having nice holidays in the country every year, having a good life' – which would be amusing were it not for the consequences it might have had.

Decisions

Around one in four applicants are refused asylum on 'non-compliance' grounds, that is, failing to return their Statement of Evidence Form within the 14 days. Reputable advisers agree that some clients are refused on non-compliance grounds even when their SEF *is* returned in time.

At the Tamil Welfare Association in Newham caseworkers always send in the completed SEF by special delivery. However, they were able to show us a dozen examples of refusals on the grounds that the document had not been received. Their next move, they explained, was to lodge an appeal, after which the Home Office would go back on their refusal and offer to reconsider the application.

A Zimbabwean interviewee had been rightly advised to keep a record of posting his SEF. He too received a refusal on non-compliance grounds. 'But the application was in time,' he said. 'It was sent registered delivery.' He felt there was no point complaining. 'To whom shall I complain?'

A handful of interviewees had been refused asylum without having been interviewed (which is against the rules). All of them found this deeply distressing. One, from Iran, told us despairingly:

> 'Without attending an interview, they refused me. Who's responsible in this matter? I don't know. They have wasted my right. They have wasted my chance.'

However, the majority of those we talked to who never had an interview were eventually granted permission to stay – though at the time we met them they felt completely in the dark, puzzled and anxious at not having had an interview.

Many asylum applicants find it difficult to understand, let alone accept, the reasons given in Home Office refusal letters. They feel their cases are self-evident and are surprised and shocked at the obstacles put in their way. An Iranian survivor of torture remarked: 'Verification, lawyers, documents. No one told me that these were the important things.' Some refugees who have been in the UK for many years speak of the growth of a 'culture of disbelief' and of the Home Office not wanting to know or understand. A woman from a wealthy family in Algeria also voiced this concern:

'What's happening in a country – the conflicts and dangers – surely that comes into consideration? They said I'm here because of economic reasons. I swear it: my family don't even know that I am a refugee.'

We also met Iraqi Kurds facing a situation similar to that of the Czech Roma who commented: 'Everybody knows, politicians know, what's going on in the Czech Republic. Racism ... So I think, they know, so I was surprised [that] Immigration is against us.'

People working directly with asylum hopefuls commented on how often they found a refusal was based on a relatively insignificant detail while the main thrust of the claim was ignored. On the other hand, asylum claimants given a positive decision by the Home Office received no indication as to why, as it is not Home Office practice to give reasons for allowing people to stay. The system appears to be without transparent assessment criteria.

Asylum decisions are in theory taken on an individual basis. In practice, the evidence shows that the nationality of the applicant weighs heaviest. At the time of our interviews, Iraqi Kurds were receiving negative decisions, and many of those we met spoke of their refusal as though it were automatic ('I got my refusal', not 'I got a refusal'). Not long before, however, Iraqi Kurds had been receiving positive decisions. Afghans, on the other hand, were receiving what seemed like automatic positive decisions, often without being interviewed. Among those people dispersed to Glasgow – many of whom were from Afghanistan – the acceptance rate on a first decision reached 80 per cent or more, compared to an average overall of around 30 per cent. Yet some nationalities – notably the east European Roma – appear to be routinely refused.

Waiting

The majority of those seeking asylum suffer long waits, typically for an appeal after being refused asylum. The argument for faster initial decisions is meritorious, though this would simply move the bottleneck further along the line as the backlog for appeals builds up. The strain is particularly acute outside London, and although many more adjudicators were appointed in 2001–2, the wait for appeal remains very long. If and when it becomes much shorter, as intended, it is unlikely that conscientious lawyers will be able to keep up with the volume of work unless the entire system becomes much more efficient. More appellants will be badly represented, or unrepresented, which will further curtail their chances of finding safety.

Among those of our interviewees who had been in Britain for a considerable time, some were still awaiting even an initial decision. They appeared to be part of an unfortunate group 'in the middle' who had not been in Britain long enough to qualify for virtually automatic acceptance under the 'backlog clearance',[2] yet were not among the relatively recent arrivals who get speeded-up decisions. Yet the interviewees in this category appeared to have strong cases: many were well integrated and for the most part employed, often in asylum support organizations as interpreters or caseworkers.

Typical among such applicants would be people like K. He arrived from Sudan four years before we interviewed him but had had no decision on his claim. Like others in a similar position he felt he was owed a positive decision, both because of his history in his own country, and because he was contributing in the UK:

'Why do I not have a positive decision? I'm involved in the community, working, paying tax ... All my life is on stop. I can't go on holiday; I can't get a mortgage, can't travel ... I can't buy a car, can't meet a wife, have children, get on with my life, get on with anything.'

He was one of those who refused to 'cheat' by winning permission to stay through a marriage of convenience with a British national.

An Iranian man we met in Glasgow suffered from a lack of basic necessities while waiting for an answer from the Immigration Service:

'I am just waiting. Usually people have to wait ... six months. I cannot go to work, because I don't have a licence ... At the moment I am suffering about money. I want to buy some things very necessary – tee-shirt, shoes. I get just £10 a week cash. Vouchers, I have to use [a] £5 [voucher]. They give no change. This is robbery. 15p. 19p. They keep it.'

This experience of life being 'on hold' – a consequence of waiting for a first decision, for an appeal result or for the papers following a successful final outcome – was described by some asylum applicants as 'insufferable'.

Appeals

In 2001, one in four appeals was upheld, up from around one in five the previous year.[3] Some experienced immigration lawyers have suggested that this rise was a direct result of first decisions being reached which increasingly sacrificed quality for speed.

Among the applicants we met, most were still awaiting the results of their appeals, having received initial negative decisions; among them were torture victims with medical evidence to back their claims. They won eventually, but only after several adjournments. Attending their appeals, one was left wondering how seriously the Home Office had considered their claims. In a couple of cases the Immigration Department had not produced a Home Office Presenting Officer to argue its case before the adjudicator, suggesting it had decided its refusal was not defensible.

Though some adjudicators could be sympathetic, a lack of consistency among them was another repeated concern. Some lawyers clearly held the view that success or otherwise at appeal depends a great deal on who hears it. Some adjudicators had a reputation for turning down appeals whatever the evidence, while others were held to be objective and fair-minded.

The conclusion reached by a number of interviewees and those who represent them is that the whole process is a gamble. An 18-year-old Kosovan awaiting his appeal adopted that very terminology, adding:

'They don't bother to read your case, it's just luck, pure luck. If they like your name, they'll give it to you! I don't think I've been lucky this far.'

CHAPTER FOUR

Captives

'On the cell door it was written, "Deportee". I questioned it. "It doesn't matter," they said. "I'm *not* a deportee," I said. "Detainee, deportee – it's the same," they said.' (*Detainee, Cardiff Prison*)

'I was in prison and you visited me.' (Matthew 25.36)

Some countries in western Europe have powers to detain people seeking asylum without legal time limits. Some have powers to detain them without judicial oversight. Britain is alone in claiming the power to hold them both without prescribed time limits and without automatic judicial review. Unlike criminal suspects, asylum applicants are neither charged nor tried: they are effectively held captive. This situation is viewed with surprise in mainland Europe though in the UK it appears to arouse very little concern.

Detainees in Britain may seek release on bail, but this requires a knowledgeable and conscientious lawyer, and not all have access to one. Unlike prisoners charged with a criminal offence, they do not enjoy a presumption of liberty. At any one time there will be a small number who will have been locked up for a year or even two. During the period of our research at least two had been detained for two and a half years.

Administrative detention, a little-known part of British law, is a discretionary power that has to date applied to immigrants. It is implemented under the Immigration Act 1971, and was envisaged as a measure for permitting the short-term detention of illegal entrants, normally an overnight deprivation of liberty. From around the mid-1980s, as asylum claims increased, so did the periods spent in detention under Immigration Act powers. But the Act was not devised for a world of mass migration, still less for a world where substantial numbers come seeking asylum.

In recent years the British Government has expanded its capacity to detain asylum claimants. In October 2001 Home Secretary David Blunkett announced plans to increase detention places by 110 per cent by the year 2003. The following month, with the profound implications of the 11 September atrocities in the United States, the Government announced its intent to hold suspected terrorists (including people seeking asylum) indefinitely, without judicial review in the High Court. Having derogated from

Article 5 of the European Convention on Human Rights 1953 (ECHR), the Home Secretary denied that this amounted to internment. Other European states found no need to suspend civil liberties on a similar scale.

The detention of asylum claimants had already increased fourfold in the decade that preceded the Home Secretary's announcement of further capacity. This decade had seen four major pieces of legislation on asylum and immigration, though arguably only the most recent, the Nationality, Immigration and Asylum Act 2002, furthered the provision acknowledged in the 1999 Act, for regulations and safeguards commensurate with the increasing use of detention. Such regulations were needed since guarantees against arbitrary detention had been enshrined in British law under the Human Rights Act 1998, which incorporated the ECHR.

The 1999 Act included a presumption of liberty for detainees, as is enjoyed by criminal defendants, but since it was hedged around with a number of exceptions some critics regarded it as meaningless. The 2002 Act overturned this provision, and proposed increased detention places. In addition, bail continued to be conditional, with the conditions, including substantial sureties and a fixed address, remaining beyond the reach of most newly arrived asylum claimants. Accordingly, the 2002 Act removed the provision for automatic bail hearings set out in the 1999 Act that was never implemented. Arguably the only significant concession made by the 1999 Act was the granting of legal aid for representation at bail hearings.[1]

The Government's expansion of detention places, known as 'removal centres' under the 2002 Act, is meant to expedite removal of failed asylum applicants. At the time of this announcement in 2001, at least 50 per cent of all people seeking asylum were incarcerated *before* the outcome of their claim was settled, not at the end of the legal process. Critics of the system argue that a significant change in practice is required if the pattern of detention on arrival is to be shifted sufficiently to warrant calling detention centres 'removal centres'.

Although it had been official policy not to use ordinary prisons to lock up people seeking asylum, by late 2001 two-thirds of all asylum detainees were still being held in prison. This number fell during 2002 as new 'dedicated' detention places were made available, and it was claimed that the practice had been discontinued.[2]

Successive governments have given broadly similar reasons for detaining asylum applicants: they are held only as a last resort and for the shortest possible period, usually only as appropriate to effect removal, initially to establish the basis of a person's claim or identity, or where there are grounds for believing that the person will not abide by any conditions attached to the grant of temporary admission or release.

Research conducted by the University of Cambridge Institute of Criminology in 2000[3] found that official guidelines carried less weight in decisions to detain than the availability of detention space: different ports had widely varying levels of detention. This research also noted 'goal shift', 'where detention has come to be used systematically for general deterrence and to expedite processing, and in an *ad hoc* fashion to encourage withdrawal of applications'. The operational guidelines governing detention state that 'the aim should be to free detention space for those who have shown a *real* disregard for the immigration laws *and* who are able to be removed within a realistic timescale'.[4]

The number of people detained each year is not known. It is possible the Home Office does not have such figures: certainly it never publishes them, preferring instead to give 'snapshot' figures which tell the number held on any one day.[5] The Refugee Council found in 1997 that 10 per cent of those who claimed asylum on arrival at Heathrow, Gatwick, Dover or other ports of entry were detained immediately.[6] An organization called Bail for Immigration Detainees calculated in 1999 that more than 10,000 people seeking asylum are detained each year, and numbers have increased since.

Whatever the figures, there is evidence that certain nationalities are more likely to be detained than others. Roma, for example, are automatically detained, and in 2001–2 the practice was applied conspicuously to black Zimbabweans. Asylum applicants from the former Soviet Union and central Europe are also routinely held. Oakington Detention Centre, near Cambridge, holds applicants from 'designated' countries – countries whose nationals are assumed not to have valid claims – for a week while their cases are 'fast-tracked'. Most of the detainees we interviewed came from countries on the designated list, though none of their claims could have been considered manifestly unfounded.

Sixteen of our interviewees had been detained for a month or more. Three others – all women – had been held for one week only in the 'fast-track' Oakington centre. We interviewed all 19 after their release, 3 within a fortnight of their release. Most were living in London although 3 were in Dover, 1 in Havant (Hampshire), 1 in Sheffield and 3 in Glasgow. We met them all through members of voluntary organizations.

Of the 16 who had been held for a month or more:

- 10 had been detained in prison;
- 6 had been detained in a dedicated detention centre;
- 3 had been in both;
- 1 had been in no fewer than three prisons, finishing in top-security Belmarsh.

Twelve of the 16 were detained on arrival, 3 within a few months of arrival, 1 after nearly two years.

Of the 3 detainees who had been released after one week in Oakington, 2 had been dispersed to Glasgow having had 'fast-track' refusals. They were awaiting their appeal. The third had given up pursuing her case because she thought the legal fees would be too much. She was living in London, supported by a sister. The total duration of detention ranged from 32 days to 14 months, with the mean average just under 6 months.

Ten of the 16 were Africans, 4 were Roma from the Czech Republic, 1 was Romanian (not Roma Gypsy), and 1 a Tamil from Sri Lanka. Among the 3 women who were released after being held for a week in Oakington, 2 were from Zimbabwe and 1 was a Roma from the Czech Republic. Most of the detainees were in their twenties.

Nine of the interviewees gave details of health problems. Of these, 7 recounted experiences of torture. One, the only woman among the16, had been multiply raped. When put in the context of other research, 7 torture victims out of a total of 16 detainees turns out not to be exceptional (for example, the sole published UK survey of the mental health of asylum detainees includes interviews with 15 detainees (all men), of whom 4 had a history of torture and 1 of rape).[7]

Our findings add to the body of existing evidence that detention of people seeking asylum in the UK is arbitrary and against international human rights standards, in particular the European Convention on Human Rights incorporated into UK law as the Human Rights Act 1998. The 'information vacuum' identified by Pourgourides remains just as acute and continues to cause mental anguish and mental illness in asylum detainees. Our findings also support research conducted by the Medical Foundation for the Care of Victims of Torture, which demonstrates that the Home Office has no systems in place for ensuring that torture victims do not suffer detention in the UK.

The experiences of our interviewees demonstrate that whether or not a claimant has been tortured has little or no impact on the decision to detain. Our interviews also endorsed the findings of the Medical Foundation that, even where a history of torture is established, the torture survivor continues to be detained. On the basis of cases they examined between January 1999 and June 2000, the Medical Foundation asked whether the undertaking the Government made in the White Paper *Fairer, Faster and Firmer*[8] – that a history of torture should weigh strongly in favour of temporary admission – was being taken at all seriously. Our research leads us to suggest the answer to this question must remain 'no'.

Several of our interviews underline a point the authorities themselves recognize, that prison is not the place to which asylum applicants should be sent. This has been said many times before, but what is new here is that the evidence comes directly from the people most concerned, the detainees themselves. In addition, these first-hand accounts offer evidence to support a claim that has long been made, that deprivation of liberty is used as a means of coercing detainees to return home 'voluntarily'. This deterrent purpose is forbidden by the Immigration Service's own rules and is in direct defiance of international law.

The experiences related by our interviewees suggest a worrying lack of concern in some official circles about the suffering of innocent people who have simply asked, as they are entitled to do, for this country's protection. Such treatment of fellow human beings is not compatible with Christian principles as recognized by CTBI, nor indeed with any civilized response to displaced people arriving in Britain.

Arrival

The prevailing practice and procedures asylum applicants meet on arrival are illustrated in the series of stories below, some of which were given in anger by interviewees. Delays, a lack of legal representation and carelessness are only the tip of an almost inhuman iceberg for those seeking refuge.

> 'They stopped me, I stay in Heathrow. I got there at 8 a.m., had an interview at 4.30 pm. Two and a half hours. There was no solicitor. I didn't know what to say or do. I explain everything. I said, "Don't send me back home, send me to Canada." The guy interview me, he was polite, but he was kind of busy. He said, "Wait here." He kept going up and down: "Wait here," he said, and he'd just go and come back. I didn't eat … After the interview they say they're going to find me a place. Six o'clock they take me to Queen's Building in Heathrow. I did five days there, sleeping with my luggage … After that they send me to come, they tell me, "Pack your luggage, you're going somewhere." I didn't know England, no people, so they take me to JA [one of the buildings in Harmondsworth Detention Centre near Heathrow]. I tell them I'm an asylum seeker, they do papers, they give me a copy. So I went to JA for seven and a half months. The judge in the first court said, "You didn't have a solicitor at your interview? You should have had one."' (*Torture survivor*)

Of Oakington Detention Centre – the fast-track deportation facility – one said:

> 'I didn't particularly like the place, though it was quite decent. At that time they explained to us after seven days you'll be given a decent

place to stay. Also I had a substantive interview. I had a lawyer [*private, from outside*]. The decision was based on what I went through with them. I was refused. The whole process was very rushed. You can only answer the questions asked. It was streamlined. You can't answer a question if it hasn't been asked. You can only answer questions they ask – e.g. according to what the interviewer wanted to hear, not how you wanted to express it yourself. Two days later – refusal. There were no acceptances while I was there. Quite a lot were Zimbabweans.' [*This interviewee was moved to prison.*]

The point raised by this interviewee was also made to us by lawyers. One wrote that 'from the beginning of the interview the interviewing officer asked questions at a very high speed, often cutting short Mr T's answer in a quite abrupt manner, and moving on to new topics'. Interpretation can also be an issue at Oakington: for example, we came across a case of an Albanian who discovered after his interview that his interpreter was a member of an opposing political group. He claimed that the notes of his interview did not reflect what he had said. Interviews cannot be repeated.

Detention centre or prison?

Following a major lobby by NGOs, the Home Office ceased detaining people seeking asylum in prison, but after a fire destroyed much of Yarl's Wood Detention Centre in Bedford, the authorities reverted to detaining people in prisons again.[9] The stories recounted here, therefore, reflect the experiences of detainees who corroborate visitors' reports that the conditions in detention centres are very similar to those in prison. One detainee told us:

'There were eight people accompanying us. A hell of a security exercise there. Too much. When the vehicle stops, you're taken one at a time into the prison. Two prison officers, they open the door, take one of us, then lock it. Then you were locked in a cell. Security check, on admission you are told to strip. You have to strip to your birthday suit. You're made to squat. Two people, one Ugandan, one Zimbabwean, had random drugs tests. Negative. They take a sample of urine. Then you put on your clothes, go for X-ray. Metal detector. Like in airports. You're called one at a time. For admission procedures. Photographs (fingerprints have been taken already). They open a file, given prison number. It's not your fault, it's the regulations. If immigration would only put something in writing, as to what are our rights … I have suffered so much. This is what I've been waiting for [to talk about what happens].'

We were told of other experiences:

'We went through the process, signed in, ID cards, given prison clothes, uniform. You're not allowed to wear your own clothes. When you change into prison clothes, you strip off in front of the guards. I felt bad about that. The first day, you get to see a doctor. Not a medical, just ask have you been in prison before? Any allergies?'

'They check [you] naked, checking for drugs. [You] just come to ask asylum, they treat you like criminal. When they say this is good place is not, is bad. The way they treat asylum seekers is not good, like animal, like people have no dignity. They put them in the corner, they're not a priority. Immigration, Home Office, you know all the cases won't be accepted, but you've got to tell people before – if you don't want me, tell me. Not wait, six, seven months [in prison], then tell me.'

'These conditions are very damaging. Seventy people on the wing, sharing about five showers. Bare feet. People spitting on the floor. Someone was caught masturbating in the shower. It was running from that end all over the floor. One of my friends managed to assist in the kitchen. He told me they used bathroom towels to clean the trays and utensils. That's wrong. We're not used to that. In the cells the toilets … are open. Not disinfected. The cells [are] 7 feet by 14 feet. I measured it myself. We were two in my cell. Toilet in corner, basin. That's the dining room too. Where you eat. No disinfectant. Someone can use the toilet while you're eating. There's a small window at the top – not enough to ventilate the cell. I was sharing with a guy from my country. We could make arrangements, avoid using the toilet unless very desperate. When you were out for food, you'd try to sneak into the toilet [on the wing], but usually they lock it up to stop us – except in Association. Sometimes I went 48 hours without using the toilet. I used to lie on my stomach. There was no spray. One of our friends was sharing the same cell with an asthmatic – sick, sick – he couldn't finish a sentence without gasping for air. He was from Ghana. A week before I left he went to the hospital. Asthmatics need fresh air. It's wrong to put him in such a confined environment.'

'One man was put in solitary because of lack of communication. Albanian. He was asking to go to his cell. The warders are not trained for asylum seekers. In their eyes if you're a prisoner, you have committed some crime. They thought he was refusing to cooperate, being insolent. He was taken to the [segregation] block ... That means no gym, no exercise.'

'Voluntary' return

'We wanted to find about what going to happen. They offered voluntary return forms, the prison officers, the first day. You were asked if you'd changed your mind about going home. Some did crack. Most of them were Kosovars. They weren't even staying for two weeks. They went back.'

'Immigration makes a visit to the prison every Monday, Wednesday, Friday. He says, "Are you ready to leave?" The papers are there. A lot of people were signing to go. There was a Colombian guy, two Albanians, one Indian – that's just who I remember. There were lots more. They sign, in the absence of their solicitors and withdraw their case. You have to book an appointment with Immigration before – if you don't give a reason, they won't book you. "Reason?" he [prison officer] asks. Answer: "Wants to sign." Then you get your appointment. When you're taken to prison, they expect you to surrender and say "Let me go [home]." It's a sort of torture, designed to make you give up.'

'I guess at the time I was getting used to the idea of being sent back home. That seemed to be the only way out of the situation. If I had? That's the one thing I couldn't face. If I felt safe, I would have gone voluntarily. But I didn't. There wasn't [physical] pressure. The pressure was mainly psychological.'

CHAPTER FIVE

Support

'We want someone to listen to us; it is a relief when you talk what you feel.'
(*Somali woman, London*)

'But we have this treasure in clay jars, so that it may be made clear that
this extraordinary power belongs to God and does not come from us.'
(2 Corinthians 4.7)

The Churches believe that the Government's approach to asylum policy
should be founded on cardinal values and moral imperatives, the bases on
which all human life is treated as sacred. To this end, the maxim that everyone
is innocent until proven guilty would be respected, and policy would be
consistent with the biblical affirmation that all persons are created equal in
the image of God (Genesis 1.27; Mark 10.6).

Dignity and worth

On this basis, we are mandated to uphold the dignity and infinite worth of
every individual, and, of course, of the stranger, regardless of nationality,
ethnicity, culture, sex, age, colour or religion. Any provision of support, therefore, including standards of accommodation, should acknowledge that
personal safety and physical security are vital in law and should be practised
by all institutions.

Much debate has been focused on government plans to detain asylum
applicants in accommodation centres.[1] This has diverted attention from the
fact that the vast majority of those seeking asylum will, for the foreseeable
future, depend on accommodation and support under the dispersal system
introduced in the 1999 Immigration and Asylum Act.

Four pilot accommodation centres are proposed before others are built.
The body in charge of organizing and managing dispersal, the National
Asylum Support Service (NASS), will run these. However, since both the
pilots and the centres themselves will be unable to meet the anticipated rise
in demand, and controversy surrounds their size and location, asylum applicants will continue to be dispersed to areas outside London and the south-
east, wherever low-cost (often hard-to-let) accommodation is most plentiful.

The proportion being dispersed may also increase due to government
plans to close the option of receiving support only, without accommodation.

If asylum applicants may not live with family or friends without forfeiting support, the hardship for them and their hosts will be severe. More will be forced into accommodation not of their choice in cities away from their own communities.

Dispersal was meant to be a brief stay (not more than a week) in temporary accommodation on arrival. Allocation was to be on a basis of linguistic and cultural 'clusters', so that asylum applicants from the same background would be together and interpreting would be made simpler. In practice, however, 'temporary accommodation' can last months. Such conditions are often crowded, insecure and inappropriate, with inadequate food and offering little privacy. Children in 'temporary' accommodation have difficulty getting into local schools, and GPs will not accept 'temporary' people as patients. Many of the people we interviewed spoke disparagingly of their experiences in temporary – particularly hostel – accommodation. (The one exception was the hostel in the Folkestone Road, Dover, which was inspected regularly by Migrant Helpline. The staff there made the atmosphere welcoming, and, unusually for temporary accommodation, no one in charge prevented us having a look round.)

This comment from an Iraqi Kurdish woman is typical:

'We spent one night in Dover, then we came to Merton … We were five months in temporary accommodation, that was the worst part. It was horrible – my daughter had medical problems because of it. We shared a bathroom and toilet with 16 families. My daughter refused to use the toilet and got constipated. The GP said she had to go to hospital, they thought they would have to make an operation. We had our flat [just] in the right time … [She is] five.'

An asylum seeker from Kurdish Iraq spoke of having 'one room in a hotel':

'I can't cook in it, we share a bathroom, in filthy conditions, you have to be in time, have to come back before 10 p.m. and you can't leave before certain times. It wasn't a very nice place.'

Social Services accommodation has received far less attention than accommodation under the NASS, but is often no better:

'The Social Services found my house, it's not all right. I have too much water in my sons' bedroom. I have tried to speak too many times, but nothing changes. My big son's bedroom is very small. He shares it with my small son. My young son was sleeping with me, but he's big now. There was just my bed and another small bed for my big son. Then the English people that I met in the church came in my house

and give me a bunk bed. They help me too much ... I don't like to disturb [the Social Services] too much. Maybe it's my mistake. If I have a problem, I try to sort it out, but this time maybe there's no solution ... Many times my young son say to me, "Why you don't change?" I have fright if I try and change my home they bring me in a hostel. I say my son, it's very good, stay here and don't talk nothing.'
(*Kosovan female, Leyton*)

Major problems occur when applicants are separated from lawyers and when there is unavailability of lawyers in dispersal areas outside London. This is compounded when there is a lack of communication between NASS, local authorities and the Immigration and Nationality Department's asylum team. Moreover, when applicants successfully gain asylum they will often find themselves homeless and destitute. NASS is informed of the decision and duly cuts off support within a fortnight. However, the documents to activate mainstream benefits and housing rights for the successful candidates can take weeks and even months to be issued. We came across examples of claimants becoming homeless *after* being granted asylum, and the experi- ence of this 21-year-old woman from Sierra Leone may not be untypical:

'Since I had ELR, Income Support stops. I had to apply for Jobseeker's Allowance, but for 2 or 3 weeks, you have to survive on what you can. Automatically, when the Home Office gives you ELR, they tell them to stop your benefits, but [the Benefits Agency] say you need documents [before they give you Jobseeker's Allowance]. If they can stop the Income Support so quickly, why can't they send out the documents so quickly? It's a strain, stressful as well. It's all help, but still ... I really want to study and move on.'

In the 2002 Act, the Government withdrew support from applicants who lodge their claim after leaving the port of entry, so-called in-country applicants. A High Court judge has ruled, however, that the Home Office was putting the lives of six applicants in this category at risk of 'injury or death', and breaching the European Convention on Human Rights. The Government lost its appeal to have this judgement overturned.

Many asylum applicants said that they felt safer in London, where there are many different nationalities and where they did not stand out, than in those dispersal areas where immigrants are unfamiliar. (A Government con- cession in the 1999 Act was that torture-survivors who are patients of the Medical Foundation should be allowed to stay in London. In practice, this doesn't always happen.) One Venezuelan man we interviewed in London told us that, while he didn't feel 'the English' supported him, at least 'they're not attacking either. Here the police protect the [Hare Krishna] temple, especially after football days: when West Ham United play, there are police around the temple.'

The police were also commended by a Palestinian man in Plymouth, who told us:

> 'I trust the police ... One person in the house was mentally ill. They took him to the hospital for a week, but there was a bad interpreter and they didn't explain to him that he would be let out only for a few hours each day. So he came back to the house. The hospital called the police and they came [to] the house to search for him. I worked with the police and took him back to the hospital with them. The police talked very nicely to him.'

CCRJ has consistently maintained that families should not be broken up, either through deportation or dispersal, as this can cause deep distress. Siblings should always be kept together, but family members outside the 'nuclear' family, like cousins, may be separated. Often, however, children will have travelled together, supported each other, and need to stay together. Moreover, a cousin or close friend may be the only person a child knows. Separation then is very cruel. On the other hand, social workers are very wary of claimed relationships between a minor and someone older who may not be related, and may do the minor harm (for example, as a trafficker or in league with traffickers. Sometimes, social workers have told us, minors themselves may be involved in trafficking.) A 21-year-old woman from Sierra Leone, now based in London, related her experience:

> 'I came with my sister and two of my cousins. They separated us, my cousins are in Sheffield, because of the housing, really. There's a law about asylum seekers to send them away from London. We lost everything, only my cousins that were left, family died. It's only because of my age that I'm here [in London]. My sister is just 16. My cousins are away. Especially [it is bad for] her, she's been through a lot, she's especially upset about my cousins, only me and them she's got.'

We also heard of a Roma family who were put on different buses upon their arrival at Dover: the grandmother was sent to Manchester, the husband and other males to detention in Liverpool, and the rest of the family to Hastings. When the men were let out they went to Manchester and the rest of the family eventually left Hastings to travel there too. A hostel worker told us that in his experience the Home Office 'are always separating families: they just can't be bothered to keep them together'.

Sighthill

Many people seeking asylum resent being transferred to localities in which temporary accommodation is situated, as it is often run-down, badly serviced and densely populated by socially deprived and excluded people. One individual we spoke to in Sighthill, Glasgow, told us he had been attacked, and that another had been murdered in that area two years before. The man also spoke of his shock at the local culture, notably the widespread use of drugs by young people.

In Glasgow the availability of hard-to-let council accommodation has led to claimants being placed in high-rise blocks in very run-down areas like Sighthill. Though the area was dangerous, the flats had been freshly painted and equipped with white goods and furniture. This caused great resentment among local residents, who thought that the asylum seekers were getting a better deal from the council than they. New cookers, fridges and washing machines that had been moved into a flat in advance of its occupation by asylum applicants had often been stolen by the afternoon, so delivery was now held back until flats were occupied.

Another problem in Sighthill was that the 250 Kurds housed there faced an hour and a half's walk every Friday to a mosque. When asked to help, a local minister arranged for a (nearer) Catholic church to be 'converted' for their use.

While some attacks on immigrants are racially motivated, people seeking asylum do not class all British people as 'racist'. Some have had very positive experiences with local people, and we came across many examples of asylum hopefuls who had received a welcome from neighbours, help with finding their way around, and invitations to attend or participate in events. We heard of an evening in a nightclub where locals and refugees ended up joining in a Kurdish dance. Havens run by voluntary groups including churches offer food, advice and, in some cases, English language classes.

Education and health

With such a low premium placed on the value of asylum claimants, constant relocation can affect children's schooling, and some claimants we spoke to were concerned about the limited opportunities for their children to be formally educated. One Iraqi Kurd mother said it took five months for her to get a place in a school for her children, and a Tamil woman from Sri Lanka, with sons aged six and twelve, commented that 'just a *day* in school is a great thing'. A county council Social Services team told us that many schools would not take children of asylum seekers in case it adversely affected their league table ratings. To overcome the problem the council decided that schools taking the children of asylum applicants would not have their ratings changed. 'So now we're left with the basic prejudice' as a bar to entry, a member of the team commented. Some applicants understood that the standard of education their children might enjoy here was less rigorous than in their home countries, and some indicated that their children had been bullied, though there was much praise for teachers. It is not always recognized that the frequent movement of pupils is disruptive for teaching staff and children as it destroys continuity.

Access to college is also difficult. 'Families who are in the appeals process don't have the right to go to college', a refugee woman now working for the Migrant Organization in London told us:

> 'A client lost two years because his family was in the appeals process. He was 18, he wanted to go to college, he got a place, but when he went to register, the college demanded papers, and they showed that he was in a Home Office appeal, so they said, no, sorry, there is no place until your case has been decided. I was so angry, I went to the college and I convinced them to take him, I pointed out that to leave a boy out on the streets at this age is very dangerous. Organized crime – he could be appropriated by drug dealers and criminals. So he was registered, then after two weeks, they said he hadn't paid, the registration was only temporary, and he was expelled from the college. After one year, he got a decision. Now he's unstable, he goes to college, but he doesn't feel at ease there, he needs counselling, but that is difficult nowadays as well. According to the law, you do have the right to go to college while you're in process, but colleges are breaking the law.'

Obtaining access to health care can also prove difficult for people in temporary accommodation seeking asylum. In some cases local GPs can be less than cooperative. The following are two of the most harrowing stories we came across:

> 'Even when you go to the GP, they don't take you. We want someone to listen to us, it is a relief when you talk what you feel. "You are asylum seeker", they are telling us – when they say this word, we suffer a lot. You can understand from their eyes. Lastly, when I got my paper, I looking for accommodation, I went to GP to get some help [a letter to housing explaining her health needs], I was suffering depression, every week I was going to counsellors, I did two kinds of operation on this country. The GP said, "Why are you asking?" He doesn't want to write letters.' (*Somali woman, London*)

'My wife had 10 January pregnancy. But after [a negative decision on their asylum claim] she lost the baby. We went to the hospital – we had no money to get back [they were living on vouchers]. [At] 2.00 a.m. in the morning we came on foot. One and a half hours. We asked for an ambulance because my wife can't walk, even they refused. Even we didn't have an interpreter. We always have problems getting to hospital and returning.' (*Iranian Kurd male, Leeds*)

However, there were also some positive stories:

'[I am] very satisfied with health service, very helpful. Got problems with eye, little boy, they did it, looked after him, fantastic, can't fault it. If it had happened in Czech Republic, he'd be blind by now. [My wife's] father had operation in the Czech Republic to remove cataracts [which is what the little boy has got], they did it badly, he's blind now. Over here, such good care. Cousin with cataracts, he's made appointment with specialist. Every two weeks his son's eyes are checked and it helps.' (*Romany male, Dover*)

Vouchers have now been abolished, but the suffering and exclusion they caused need to be noted. Many asylum claimants spoke of the humiliation they felt, and of the iniquity of the system that prevented them being given change when they tendered vouchers. Some local authorities issued vouchers, some with no cash element at all, and some only for exchange in certain specified supermarkets. This exemplifies a fundamental need for effective integration of people seeking asylum in the UK.

CHAPTER SIX

Integration

'We don't want to be asylum seekers; we want to work.' (*Palestinian woman, Hull*)

'The Lord watches over the strangers; he upholds the orphan and the widow.' (Psalm 146.9)

The Churches promote and discharge racial justice work in the belief that all people belong to one race, the human race; but naturally CCRJ recognizes different ethnicities or people groups. One of the criticisms often levelled at the United Kingdom's immigration policy and practice is the shortsightedness that prohibits integration. Many who seek asylum, it is argued, could contribute much to the economy, culture and well-being of the country if they were helped to integrate into society and allowed to work instead of being harassed with threats of deportation. A refugee worker in Redbridge, East London, told us that even to think of a long-term orientation or integration programme is a 'complete luxury' since basic needs such as shelter, food and benefits have to be sorted first. He found that Social Services departments do not refer clients, and are often displeased when clients are given information or help to access their entitlements.

The dignity of work

As part of the creation narrative and therefore as something that, in an important way, helps to make us human, it is vital to recognize how important work is thought to be to God in the Judaeo-Christian tradition. Whilst it gives us purpose, fulfilment, worth and satisfaction, in working we are also co-creating with God. We met many applicants with an apparently profound commitment to achieving qualifications and finding work, but who were thwarted at every turn. Some already had qualifications but were unable, for various reasons, to obtain suitable employment.

An Iraqi woman living in South London is an example of the latter. She told us that she was a university lecturer in civil engineering in her home country. She also obtained her MSc in Iraq,

'but here they don't recognize it. I would be delighted to work in my qualification. My husband is studying part-time for his MSc. We are on income support.'

We met a surgical nurse from Algeria at a refugee advice centre in East London who had also completed IT and office work. He had a work permit and was trying to get a job, but, he said:

'My English is not good enough. Wherever you go they ask for a minimum of two years' experience, but I don't have that here. Before, I [was] manager of the French Institute, but my boss changed and now I can't get a reference. Now I [have] 14 months' experience here. I've volunteered for 14 months, done everything: administering vouchers, doing statistics on vouchers every week, translations. I worked here three days a week until I became full-time two months ago … If I'm starting to work, I'll leave everything because I'm fed up.'

A woman from Kosovo also came up against the problem of a lack of British work experience:

'I started looking for a job in accountancy in this country, but everyone says you need experience in this country. I have experience in Kosovo accountancy. I can't get volunteer accountancy here [at the Refugee Advice Centre]. This is not equal opportunities for us. I saw an accountancy job as a junior. I could do this easy, but you need six months' experience.'

A Colombian woman now working for the Migrant Organization was a lawyer in her country. 'I worked very hard here to qualify again', she told us:

'It was a miracle that I eventually got this job. I had to live eight years on benefits, signing on every two weeks. It was very humiliating. I worked all my life in Colombia – how can they think I'm happy, facing poverty all the time? I couldn't go out, had to sign on every two weeks. You miss it once, you lose your benefits. Society thinks we're happy on benefits, but the one thing we want is work … In the Jobcentre they ask "What have you done to get a job?" You say you've looked. They say, it's not enough. You have to try harder. I got angry once: I said, "If you offer me a job *now*, I'll go." They got me a job as a cleaner. I didn't want to work as a cleaner … They got me a job as a chambermaid. I have a back problem, with a doctor's letter …'

A worker on a migrant helpline also told us that she knew of a PhD from francophone Africa who wanted to do teacher training but who was still waiting for a decision as to his status, and a medical doctor from the Congo who wanted to register as an orthopaedic surgeon and who had status but no papers.

Racism is a key factor in British society, as the Stephen Lawrence Inquiry Report found,[1] and is an added barrier to asylum applicants finding work. A Congolese woman living in Glasgow told us what happened when she applied for a part-time job:

'I applied. They said, "We'll call you." They never call. "Have you got [a] CV, experience?" No one will employ me, so where will I get experience? They say "already taken", but they keep the sign up. My white friend, she phones, they're friendly, we went to appointment, they saw black faces, they say "Sorry, the place is taken."'

The Colombian woman mentioned above experienced even more blatant discrimination, on account of both her age and her ethnicity:

'Being a woman over 50 here is a nightmare. I don't know why age here is so important. Even as nannies, the first question they ask is age. It's a prejudice. Grandmothers are very good at looking after children. Many Colombian women who are very well qualified, who study English and a profession, are still cleaning, after 100 applications. Receptionists, it's difficult too. The problem is our accent. [One employer] said the image of the company goes through the receptionist, so ... There are lots of women with mental health problems. They have no job because of their English. They're too old – it's very depressing. We used to work in our countries, [the] very [people] who [come] here used to work in their countries. Now we have to live on benefits, which is very, very depressing. People think they like it! You make the effort to be qualified ... I am a painter, I work with children. I had no work, so I registered myself as a children's teacher in painting. I saw adverts for such a post in a school. I have all the qualifications. The woman said, "Sorry, this post is only for English people." It's because parents don't like it: they prefer a good accent.'

Finding places on courses that would enhance their chances of skilled employment can also be difficult for people seeking asylum. A Rwandan living in East London told us how his plans to go to university were thwarted because of his lack of status:

'I've applied to UCAS. For university you have to be granted status – ELR and all that. I just knew this recently. I haven't called [trust funds] recently, I just wanted to find out about what to do if I fail in everything ... I like studying ... Last year I did an NVQ in Information Technology. Now I'm doing an Access to Computing [course] at W-College. It's free [but] sometimes they ask me to pay £10. I have got a counsellor at college and they have helped me a lot. If you are looking for help then you'll find it ... They've helped me write some letters to trust funds. Some of them really helped me.'

CHAPTER SEVEN

Not just a refugee

'There is nothing to live for, nothing to dream about, nothing good to think about.' (*Nigerian man, 21 years old, London*)

'If you go with us, whatever good the Lord does for us, the same we will do for you.' (Numbers 10.32)

We asked interviewees to tell us how they were occupied in their country of origin and what they were doing in Britain. What emerged from this comparison was a picture of enormous human and social waste. If the effect of asylum policy can produce such a bleak assessment of one's situation, could it be claimed that such policies undermine the critical moral value of the individual as a person? Not one of those we talked to with qualifications or skills was doing the job for which they were qualified.

The effects of inactivity

Out of 137 interviewees, no fewer than 43 were professionally qualified.

- 5 were doctors;
- 8 were teachers;
- 19 of the professionally qualified – nearly half – were working in refugee agencies, NGOs and community associations, many as interpreters
- 2 had unskilled jobs;
- 5 were unable to work because of disabling ill health or because they were responsible for dependants;
- 4 had been in the UK for less than six months, and were forbidden to work;
- 13 were unemployed;
- none of the doctors was practising;
- none of the teachers was teaching;
- all the doctors, and all but two of the teachers, had good English.

Several of the professionally qualified asylum claimants recognized that their English would hold them back, but they found that language classes they could attend were too infrequent – often only once a week – and pitched too low for them to benefit.

At the opposite end of the scale, a significant number of interviewees had previously done unskilled or casual work (often both). Several had been merely surviving – for instance, a Nigerian was selling second-hand clothes. Others had had no adult occupation except as forced recruits to a militia or guerrilla army. Five interviewees gave farming as their sole or main occupation, and a sixth owned a boat for fishing. The Roma from central Europe had lost regular manufacturing work and been forced into more marginal, precarious ways of eking out a living. But even the relatively skilled had suffered a downward slide: a Polish Roma woman, for instance, who had once been a librarian, ended up working in a shoe factory.

Eight of those whose experience put them into the broad category of 'unskilled' cared for dependants or suffered very poor health. But few regarded themselves as too sick to work. One Iraqi Kurd with an eye wound, shrapnel in his head and who described himself as 'disabled really down all one side' told us: 'I am not interested in benefits. I have worked all my life. I didn't know about them before I came.' Back home he had raised chickens and grown wheat. Here, dispersed to a northern town, he was working in a chicken-processing factory. This sort of unpopular work was easily available. In London, one Chinese interviewee was working regularly in a restaurant; another was picking up what work he could – in a restaurant if he was lucky, otherwise doing private odd jobs. Neither had permission to work.

Seven of the less skilled – all of whom had poor English – said that they wanted to work, but had not received permission. In fact, six had the right to do so because they had not received a decision on their asylum claim within six months. They were ill-informed about what they needed to do in order to obtain permission in writing. One of them had applied for permission from the Home Office, but months later was still waiting for a reply. Another was counting down the last 14 days until, he thought, he would receive what he called a 'work permit'. He did not realize that the process was not automatic, nor that he would not receive a proper permit, but merely a few words lifting work restrictions stamped on the back of the document acknow-ledging his application for asylum. The document itself made it clear that, as an asylum seeker, he was liable to detention at any time. Many asylum applicants, including several we interviewed, found that neither employers nor the Social Security offices that issue National Insurance numbers accepted this document. (The work 'concession' for asylum applicants has since been withdrawn, shutting out the possibility of legal employment.)

The occupational polarization of refugees into highly qualified on the one hand and unskilled on the other has been noted before in Home Office research. However, amongst our interviewees a striking number – some 30 in all – did not belong in either category. These included technicians (for example electricians), supervisory employees and junior managers (for instance, in quality control), clerical workers (book-keeping, administrative), artisans (carpentry, jewellery-making), skilled craftsmen (printing, welding) and men in self-employed commercial occupations (building, running a general store). In the UK, 4 in this intermediate category were employed with associations helping asylum applicants, 2 of whom were unpaid volunteers. Two had unskilled work via an employment agency (in cleaning, catering), 1 was too ill to work, whilst 9 had the right to work but were unemployed. Two technicians were not working, saying they preferred to wait for the correct documents rather than be exploited. The remainder, we understood, were also not working.

Thirteen interviewees had either been at school or been students when they left their home country. All wanted to resume their education, and 5 had started courses in further education. But unresolved asylum claims, or short-term ELR (granted only up to 18), created funding obstacles and uncertainty for the future.

Virtually all interviewees without English, or with poor English, were keen to take advantage of any available opportunity to learn. However, some who did attend courses found the fares needed to cover long distances daunting. Others lost heart while waiting to obtain a place on a course. Most of those unemployed who were studying English would have preferred more sessions a week. Some combined English with a course in IT or some other technical subject. Several of those studying regarded their lessons as a lifeline, and their tutor as their main support. (One, in Plymouth, said his teacher was his 'best friend'.) Two francophone Africans, having learnt English, were studying nursing. A couple of interviewees said they would prefer paid work to lessons if they had the choice. Three – including the Chinese – had no expectations of combining the two.

Several adults we talked to had had their education interrupted by conflict or civil war. Others had been unemployed, but this did not necessarily reflect a low standard of education, since deprivation of livelihood is a common component of persecution. A Palestinian living in Lebanon, for instance, said he had had no right to work because 'it's a political thing'. Thirty-three interviewees had been activists in their own country and regarded this as their prime vocation. Several of them, particularly women, had had no other job as 'cover'.

Deteriorating physical and mental health

Inactivity can clearly contribute to the mental and physical ill health from which so many people seeking asylum suffer. It can also add to the fear and uncertainty many feel. Yet it is only one of many factors affecting the well-being or otherwise of asylum applicants.

Many live under intense and prolonged stress. They face an accumulation of pressures and deprivations, each one of which is damaging on its
own, and which cumulatively are devastating. These include: lack of information; not being believed; fear of being refused, and of being sent back;
fear of abuse (including physical attacks); fear for family members left behind;
uncertainty; forced inactivity; dependence; poverty and exclusion; criminal-
ization; demonization in the popular press; racism; Islamophobia, notably
since 11 September 2001; disappointment; disillusionment after high hopes;
exile; loss of identity.

All of these can be sources of stress after refugees arrive in Britain, and
can in many cases increase the trauma they suffered in their countries of
origin. These may include the actual experience or threat of violence,
hazardous escape, an arduous and frightening journey, and the death or
suffering of close relatives.

Many of our interviewees spoke of having headaches and severe anxiety,
and many others were depressed. The doctors we interviewed agreed that a
high proportion of their asylum patients suffered from depression. Some
attributed it to the treatment their patients had received from the authorities.
Of four women who had been pregnant, two had had miscarriages (and one
had had to walk back from the hospital afterwards). Of the other two, one (a
Palestinian in Hull) was worried about bleeding and one had had a seven-
month emergency Caesarian section. Several had heart problems, Roma men
in particular. These may have started in the country they left, but they were
convinced the problems had got worse here.

So striking was the evidence of the damaging impact of the experience
of seeking asylum that we felt it important to try to quantify the numbers
affected.

Table 4: The health of asylum interviewees

Suffered bad health	66
Violently injured in their own country (beatings, systematic torture, or gun-shot wounds)	19
Became sick or more sick *after* their arrival in the UK	47
Symptoms that had occurred since reaching the UK (depression, bad headaches, sleeplessness)	31
Survived violence in their home country (had suffered additionally in this country, most notably those who had been detained)	47
Survived severe sexual torture and was living in 'temporary' accommodation in a hostel in London, attempted suicide both in his own country and in the UK	1

Table 4 shows how many asylum applicants felt that their health had worsened after reaching Britain. This impression is supported by more specialized research, for instance by the British Medical Association.[1]

Doctors agree that depression is a normal response to abnormal conditions and treatment. Their patients do not need drugs, just some normality in their lives and a restoration of hope. The importance of learning the language cannot be overstressed. A 25-year-old man from Iraq working with the Kent Refugee Support Group summed up the experience of many:

'Stress-related illnesses, consequences of torture, angina – they often start once they get here. How much people change over five years! Limited choices, uncertainty. Your whole life is on hold when you're awaiting a decision. Access to adult education, you want to study, or work, but you can't focus or concentrate with the waiting. Not much access, no homelessness services, food handouts and hostels. In London, there is provision for the homeless, but not here. There are no obvious hostels, evident homelessness services. You find people fighting over tiny things because pent-up anger comes out. Fights at parties. Volunteers who knew them are surprised to see people they knew fighting, because they don't realize what pent-up emotion there is. People deal with it so well – calm, polite, smiling, then they lose it.'

Since asylum applicants are usually treated by the media as a category and never shown the respect of being named, it is easy to forget that each is an individual person with his or her own story, emotions and feelings. The following quotes capture something of the anxiety many experience and where it is rooted.

'I don't know where my wife is and I don't know where my children are. Here, I go off to college and I go home. I don't have any small occupation, I don't have the right to work. I'm irresponsible about my family [*nearly in tears*]. That's how it is … [Refugee status] might give me the chance to bring my family, but as things stand, *how* can I bring my family [and] by what means? That's the problem.' (*Man from Zaire, interviewed in Plymouth*)

'At night I have bad dreams. I am waiting for bad news about my asylum claim. I am in a lot of distress. In Iran, I had a lot of problems [but] even when I arrived in England my problems are increasing day by day. My distress is increasing. What could I do?' (*Iranian man, Leeds*)

'I'm not waiting for anything except to see that mother and my sister are OK. Red Cross and Salvation Army are trying to look for them ... I go to the drop-in centre ... There is nothing to live for, nothing to dream about, nothing good to think about.' (*Nigerian man, 21 years, under appeal, London*)

'Sometimes, when the door is closed, I pray a lot and the door is open. When I need something, my immigration problem is stuck, I don't know where to go, solicitors, friends [can't help], I just close my room and start praying inside. Relax, what I want to do, I do it. I got faith. When I close my door, I pray. I believe so much the God. He's my solution. If I come to you, you're gonna help me, but you will have a limit. African and black people, they do believe a lot. They got more experience praying. Different methods of praying but one God ... I go to Catholic churches mostly, but [not always]. First of all is your faith, at the end there is just one God. You can go left or right, but there is just one God.' (*Man from Zaire, aged 29, ELR, London*)

'In the Bible, it says that God protects the widow and the orphan, and this country have the same law ... I want to see this in the practice, not only in the books.' (*Female Romanian Romany, Croydon*)

'Although we are from Africa, we too are serious and want to study. If someone like us comes, they want to put us in the [detention] centre. Unfair? If they lock people up, they can't go to school, you lose education for years in a detention centre. People have lives, just the same as they [Home Office staff] do. Everyone has a life, we've just had bad luck – we have objectives, just like they do ... The things you read in the papers. They say all asylum seekers get all the free things. That's why they think you're lying. I want to be normal, to start saving, not just to have what I live on.' (*Female from Sierra Leone, aged 21, Clapham, London*)

'It's difficult to be a refugee, it is very hard. You have to accept anything. You can't do anything. There are sometimes racial problems, but you are also neglected, they can just ignore you, tell you to come another day in the offices. They sometimes insult you, call you nigger ... It happens and you can't do anything. If you report it, you cause more problems.' (*Rwandan male, Liverpool*)

'My life is work, my mind is built up to create work. Emotional feeling, sexual feeling, you cover this problem with work. That's why I'm doing all this work.' (*Female Sudanese, London*)

'I am not ashamed to say that I am gypsy. People say – are you gypsy? Do you have a house? I say, yes, you come and see me, you knock on my door. I am not dirty, a thief. Not all gypsies are the same.' (*Romanian Romany, female, London*)

'At least I can fight. I can defend myself, this is the reason I'm not depressed or going mad. But if you don't understand English, or don't know what to do, you want to work and you don't have the chance, you go mad.' (*Female, refugee, London*)

'No way I can talk about the problems I am suffering as a result of my asylum. The loss of my children, the separation of my family. At home, our family [are] our counsellors, when you came here you have no one … Your life has changed, everything has changed.' (*Ugandan female, Romford, twelve years in UK, ELR in 1991*)

'Generally in life, you have goals, something to cling onto. If you are asylum seeker, you have nothing, you feel emptiness – you don't know where you will be. You fear for your life. Coming from such a background with community, sense of belonging, with the support of an extended family and neighbours, then you come here alone, alienated, it's really indescribable … Even to build your life from scratch is really difficult. You can't imagine – suddenly you wake up and have nothing. I've been here nearly 10 years, time goes – I cannot fit here, I cannot be there. Change, life has developed there, relationships have changed. And no matter what, I will not be part of this city. Even for children it is a problem – at school, they become like their peers, because they don't want to be different. Then they go home, to their language, their country's food, it's like two lives. My home [here], it's my country. Photos of my family, my food, it gives a sense of belonging … It's really a dilemma.' (*Sudanese female, London*)

'We have not had any racist incidents in Hull though we know the Kurds have. We can't speak to them but we do have a Kurdish family we are friendly with. We are friendly with English, Kurdish and Arab people. After that TV programme *Bloody Foreigners* I was walking through Pearson Park when an old man on a bench shouted out that I should have a good day and when I spoke to him he said that asylum seekers are welcome in Hull.' (*Palestinian female, Hull*)

'When we first arrived we were very well received because we were the first group to arrive here. I was very well received because there were not many of us. People helped us very quickly, if we wanted something they helped us at college, exercise books, pens ... But things are changing now. There were 20 people here when I arrived, now there are 400 or 500.' (*Zairean male, Plymouth*)

It seems clear from these testimonies that the Government's treatment of people seeking asylum leads to a significant deficit for them, and also for the UK. The wide range of skills and professional qualifications distributed among applicants could be put to effective use. Instead, applicants are forced to exist in ways that lead to physical and emotional ill health, which effectively leads to a cost to the public purse. In most cases this situation could be avoided if claimants were allowed to work and treated with respect whilst waiting for the outcome of their claims. But even if permission to work were granted, seekers would still face difficulty in finding appropriate work.

CHAPTER EIGHT

What future?

'I don't want to stay like this for more than one year.' (*A man from Eritrea*)

'Let mutual love continue. Do not neglect to show hospitality to strangers, for by doing that some have entertained angels without knowing it. Remember those who are in prison, as though you were in prison with them; those who are being tortured, as though you yourselves were being tortured.' (Hebrews 13.1-3)

It is clear from the experiences delineated in this report that those fleeing persecution or poverty in their own countries leave with a degree of hope that their situation will improve. Hope is intrinsic to the human condition because it implies viewing things from God's perspective. There are, therefore, certain practical aspects of hopefulness that are considered imperative. While most people seeking asylum in the UK wait for their cases to be determined, they have one overriding ambition: to learn English. This is recognized by nearly everyone as not only desirable, but a prerequisite for their future:

'I hope our situation will have improved in five years. I need to learn English – I want to be a builder.' (*Palestinian male, London*)

Most people then want to earn enough money, any way they can, to survive. They are prepared to accept the minimum wage and have low expectations about what they will be able to do here:

'I learn English. Every day I learn more. I can hear it, but expressing myself is hard. I want to continue studying, doing something with technology – aviation technology, if somebody would accept me … In my country I had a top job and I can't ask for that [in the UK].' (*Male from the Democratic Republic of Congo, Plymouth*)

'I don't think of the future here. Black economy, job market, discrimination. If they know you are an asylum seeker, they exploit you. I was given £2.45 an hour in a 24-hour shop. I was forced to do it. I can't prove that I've got academic qualifications. If I stay here [i.e. am granted asylum] I will get originals from my country …' (*Afghan male, Glasgow*)

Younger refugees – those at school – are most optimistic about their ambitions for the future:

'I would like to be a solicitor [or] some kind of computer [worker]. I like cooking like my mum. I would like to be a chef.' (*Czech Romany, aged 17, London*)

Attending college or university to study is usually part of a plan to improve one's quality of life. However, few refugees mentioned an 'ideal' job or talked about 'dreams' for their future beyond earning a wage. The career plans of those currently at college often involve working with computers (many want IT qualifications), obtaining professional qualifications (for example, in accountancy, nursing and law), and using the professional skills they already possess. Some refugees have plans to help other asylum applicants in their community, or to get involved in human rights work:

'I got NVQ level 2 in Care Assistance, then a City and Guilds Certificate as well. I went for training: it finished. Then I went for work. I worked for five months – not enough. I went for a nursing course. I'll finish it this year, then I'll go [to] university for three years. Woolwich or Kingston University. I want to do adult general nursing.' (*Male from the Democratic Republic of Congo, London*)

For some people going to university or studying is an informal type of therapy, or an alternative to the work they can't get, rather than part of a career plan, as this Kosovan woman in London shows: 'I want to live today ... I start studying at university to keep my mind busy.' Others envisage returning to their countries at some point as their biggest 'dream' for the future:

'I don't expect more than asylum ... [In the future] I'm hoping to see my country. [It would] be better to go back. I don't want to stay like this for more than one year. If I had good news from home, I go back.' (*Male from Eritrea, Glasgow*)

Others are committed to staying:

'I hope Immigration take me [in] permanent residence. I wish I'm the same as any people from England. I wish respect to the law in England, and I want cooperation with the government in law in England. But first, they have to accept me and agree with my claim.' (*Iranian man*)

For those interviewees still in the asylum system – the majority – the main preoccupation is waiting for a decision about their application. It is very draining in terms of both energy and time. By definition it means their future is uncertain, and this constrains their individual plans and increases their feeling of lack of control over their lives. Not many of the people we spoke to talked with much enthusiasm, or seemed to have a clear idea, about building a future here in the UK, although many were at college or trying to learn English. But is it really possible to have concrete plans or high-blown ambitions when you are bored with your daily life, ashamed about the conditions you live in, and embarrassed about your status as an 'asylum seeker'?

Conclusion

The stories told in these pages reflect the real experiences of people seeking asylum in the UK, and the often treacherous – in many cases fatal – paths that have led them to these islands. Indeed, it became clear from the interviews that the prevailing negative attitude fermenting in some sections of the general public, and the austere approach of Government, could not have been informed by reality. On the contrary, the depth of seekers' suffering of ill health before and after entering Britain cannot be ignored: the emotional and psychological trauma that have led to depression, and the ever-present state of anxiety in which many live because of the persistent uncertainty about deportation – sometimes after waiting for years – are not necessarily reflected in the tabloid media or some aspects of Government policy.

The Churches are clear that a more humanitarian, compassionate and fact-based response to the voices of reality in the four nations is required. What makes this crucial is the additional level of suspicion and vilification created by the threat of 'terrorism', part of which today falls unjustly and heavily on asylum applicants. CCRJ considers the following requirements absolutely vital:

1. In the light of the findings of this report, and the need to maintain absolute respect for the right of people to seek asylum, it is important that Government do all in its power to protect and maintain the effectiveness of the UN Convention on the Status of Refugees and its 1967 Protocol.
2. The Government is urged to work with other Western industrialized powers and multinational bodies to develop international policies that would address the root causes of forced migration.
3. In order to develop coherent and consistent approaches it is now necessary for Government to consider, and for Churches and the voluntary sector to lobby for, the depoliticization of asylum policy and practice by developing an accountable, multi-agency, NGO-led asylum commission. This would help to ensure awareness of humanitarian issues, deliver just decisions, reduce costs, and help Government to achieve its objectives of security and protection while promoting cohesion and inclusiveness.
4. Church congregations and leaders in the four nations are encouraged to use study materials and factual briefings to enable them to understand why people seek asylum.

5. Whilst Government and the media have a duty to inform public opinion, it is their duty also to use language in statements of fact that does not encourage abuse of refugees and immigrants either by right-wing political hate groups or others.

6. To help people seeking asylum make real contributions to society, it is imperative that the Government and the National Asylum Support Service invest seriously in improving the quality and availability of language teaching for asylum applicants and take account of research done for the DfES.

7. In recognition of the maxim that a person is innocent until proven guilty, CCRJ urges that detention should only be used in exceptional circumstances, where there is evidence of a criminal offence or a clear threat to national security.

8. There should be increased transparency in the process of determination of the claims of people seeking asylum.

APPENDIX 1

Aims and method

Aims

The objective of this work was to give a voice to, and hear stories directly from, people seeking asylum in the United Kingdom in order to inform and influence public opinion. We intended to survey the picture across a wide range of experiences, to explore refugees' and asylum claimants' specific reasons for leaving their countries of origin. We specifically set out to give each individual the opportunity to emphasize those aspects of the adventure or ordeal he or she considered most significant, enabling the voices of experience to articulate their reality freely.

Method

In order to achieve these aims, we conducted interviews with individuals and families from many different countries and ethnic backgrounds, and listened to their explanation of the circumstances that had ultimately led to their flight. The style of the interviews was conversational, and each interviewee shared opinions, hopes and aspirations whilst telling his or her story in his or her own words. We transcribed these verbatim, but respected participants' need for confidentiality.

As people seeking asylum are not normally heard in the current debate on asylum, CCRJ wanted to hear the whole story from the people directly involved. Throughout the exercise, asylum interviewees spoke of their delight at the opportunity to express themselves fully and freely. Naturally, we include in this short report only a fraction of each story, but we trust the most informative and reflective of them all.

We also interviewed legal representatives and NGOs working with asylum applicants. These included caseworkers with refugee agencies that have a role in implementing Government policy, organizers of community associations, volunteers in well-established charities, those struggling to support newly arrived asylum applicants and those who visit asylum detainees. The key criterion here was that *all had regular first-hand contact with people seeking asylum.* Many were themselves refugees who now worked in the field and offered a double perspective.

General practitioners who treat asylum applicants offered illuminating views on the impact of the asylum process on the health of their patients. The Medical Foundation for the Care of Victims of Torture contributed invaluable testimony on how the system treats torture survivors and its influence on any recovery.

Sample

To achieve these ends, we sought to obtain a sample that was in proportion to what is known of the general asylum seeker population in terms of ethnicity, nationality and gender from across the four nations. Whilst the selection of interviewees may not be regarded as a representative sample according to strict scientific data, the comparatively large and ethnically diverse number we talked to from across a wide spectrum of circumstances and political experiences from many different lands give cumulative weight and seriousness to our findings.

Access

The willingness of asylum applicants to be interviewed was dictated by two contradictory motives: distrust on the one hand, and a desire to tell their story on the other. Intermediaries were vital to the process and needed to trust both interviewers and interviewees. The interviewers were all experienced in working with people seeking asylum, and personal contacts among professionals and volunteers helped to establish the credibility of the researchers. Many contacts were refugees, and were keen to assist through interpreting. The advantages of trust and cultural affinity with interviewees outweighed linguistic difficulties.

Confidentiality

Researchers were committed to confidentiality in all cases. Interviewees had to be confident that they could tell their own stories whilst remaining unidentified. All potential interviewees were approached first by intermediaries in order to explain the project, and ascertain whether they would participate. Most interviews were arranged in advance, some were carried out on the spot, whilst others resulted from claimants who came forward to offer an interview. Many chose to be interviewed in their living accommodation.

Truth

As researchers, we were careful to inform interviewees that we had no power or authority to influence their asylum claims, and that the prime purpose of the survey was to give them a voice. A careful assessment of what people told us, including on occasion details that did not help their cases, showed that they told their stories to CCRJ with sometimes distressing integrity.

Family status in the UK

The vast majority of the interviewees were separated from their closest relatives, having left home on their own. However, 16 per cent were with their families.

Families were logged as a single unit when one member acted as spokesperson for the whole family (though others often contributed). Interestingly, in ten cases husbands and wives were interviewed together, but their experiences took different courses: two for instance had travelled separately, or they had met after arriving in the UK and had filed separate asylum claims. Where the latter had happened, these were logged as two units. Most interviewees living with a husband or a wife in the UK were seen separately, and the interview was logged as a single unit.

Churches' Commission for Racial Justice (CCRJ)

CCRJ is a Commission of Churches Together in Britain and Ireland (CTBI). Since 1971 the Churches, through CCRJ, have been engaged in monitoring trends in UK and European asylum and immigration policy and supporting and advocating on good multi-ethnic and community relations. CCRJ enables the Churches to contribute to the development of Britain's multi-ethnic, multicultural character, believing that the right to asylum reinforces and upholds the fundamental right to life and the dignity of all people, which should be respected.

Useful organizations

British Red Cross Society
9 Grosvenor Crescent
London SW1X 7EJ
020 7235 5454
email: enquiries@redcross.org.uk
www.redcross.org.uk.

The Red Cross International
Welfare Department has a family
tracing service as well as providing
assistance for family reunion. Your
local branch may provide some
relevant local service.

Catholic Bishops' Conference of England and Wales
Office for Refugee Policy
39 Eccleston Square
London SW1V 1PD
020 7834 0522 (fax: 020 7630 5166)
email: ccs@cbcew.org.uk
www.catholic-ew.org.uk

Churches' Commission for Racial Justice
Inter-Church House
35–41 Lower Marsh
London SE1 7SA
020 7523 2121 (fax: 020 7928 0010)
email: ccrj@ctbi.org.uk
www.ctbi.org.uk

Evangelical Alliance
186 Kennington Park Road
London SE11 4BT

020 7207 2100 (fax: 020 7207 2150)
email: London@eauk.org
www.eauk.org

Joint Council for the Welfare of Immigrants (JCWI)
115 Old Street
London EC1V 9RT
Advice line: 020 7251 8706, 2 p.m.
to 5 p.m. Monday, Tuesday and
Thursday
email: info@jcwi.org.uk
www.jcwi.org.uk

Medical Foundation for the Care of Victims of Torture
96–98 Grafton Road
London NW5 3EJ
020 7813 7777
email: clinical@torturecare.org.uk
www.torturecare.org.uk

Expert medical and counselling
service, including therapeutic
counselling, for refugees and
asylum applicants. Referral through
GP or self-referral. Drop-in service
1 p.m. to 4 p.m. weekdays.
Counsellors speaking the following
languages are available: Arabic
(Weds and Thurs), Farsi (Mon),
French (Tues and Fri), Kurdish
(Thurs), Lingala (Fri), Spanish (Tues),
Turkish (Weds and Fri). Otherwise
an interpreter needs to attend.

The Refugee Council
3 Bondway
London SW8 1SJ
020 7582 6922 / 7820 3000
email: info@refugeecouncil.org.uk
www.refugeecouncil.org.uk

The periodical *In Exile* gives
information about the refugee and
asylum system.

Refugee Council One Stop Service
240–250 Ferndale Road
Brixton
London SW9 8BB
020 7346 6770
Drop-in service for refugees and
asylum seekers, 9 a.m. to 5 p.m.
daily, providing advice, assistance,
hot meals, washing facilities and
medical attention.
Advice line: 020 7378 6242, open
every weekday except Thursday,
9.30 a.m. to 1 p.m.

Refugee Legal Centre
Sussex House
39–45 Bermondsey Street
London SE1 3XF
020 7827 9090
Free legal advice and
representation.
Open weekdays 8.30 a.m. to 6 p.m.
email: rlc@refugee-legal-centre.org.uk
www.refugee-legal-centre.org.uk

Refugee Support Centre
47 South Lambeth Road
Vauxhall, London SW8 1RH
020 7820 3606
Provides specialist counselling and
psychotherapy services.

Scottish Refugee Council
98 West George Street
Glasgow G2 1PJ
0141 333 1850
The national refugee agency for
Scotland.

**Shelter London NHAS Consultancy
Line**
(National Homelessness Advice
Service)
020 7242 3218
(10 a.m. to 1 p.m. and 2 p.m. to
5 p.m. every day except
Wednesday)

Welsh Refugee Council
Unit 8
William Court
Trade Street
Cardiff CF10 5DQ
email:
contactname@welshrefugeecouncil.
org

**United Nations High Commissioner
for Refugees (UNHCR)**
21–24 Millbank
London SW1 4QP
020 7828 9191
email: gbrlo@unhcr.ch
www.unhcr.ch

UNHCR organizes programmes for
refugees entering the United
Kingdom, and family reunion.
Their video pack *To Feel At Home*,
although aimed at young people, is
useful for all age groups in
understanding the plight of
refugees.

Notes

Introduction

1 ILR means Indefinite Leave to Remain and ELR means Exceptional Leave to Remain.

1 Why did you leave?

1 This figure is a small proportion of the 150 million estimated to be living outside the country of their birth. See UNHCR, *The State of the World's Refugees*, Oxford: Oxford University Press, 2000.

2 UNHCR estimates suggest there are 2 million in Iran, 2.8 million in Pakistan and 1.9 million in Sudan.

3 *United Nations Convention Relating to the Status of Refugees*, 1967, Article 3.

4 Nicola Piper, *Racism, Nationalism and Citizenship: Ethnic Minorities in Britain and Germany*, Aldershot: Ashgate, 1998.

5 Interestingly, the Refugee Legal Centre noted that nearly half of the Zimbabwean asylum seekers whom they represented in 2000–01 later won their appeal against the Home Office's refusal.

6 CCRJ works on the principle that there is only one race: the human race, but that there are different people groups, or ethnicities. The language of multiple races is divisive and militates against the intrinsic unity of the human family. We have used 'ethnic' and its derivatives in place of 'race' where appropriate in this text.

7 There is an increasing need, noted by many authorities, including the Home Department, to open up other routes in the affluent West for people seeking employment and a way to overcome the abject poverty and consequences of natural disasters in their own countries.

8 Even the Home Office can sometimes accept these grounds.

9 Justice, ILPA, ARC, *Providing Protection: Towards Fair and Effective Asylum Procedures*, London: 1997, p. 21.

10 Steve Cohen, Beth Humphries and Ed Mynott (ed.), *From Immigration Controls to Welfare Controls*, London: Routledge, 2002, pp. 13ff. See also Teresa Hayter, *Open Borders*, London: Pluto Press, 2000, pp. 8–20, for a useful account of immigration in the make-up of modern nation-states.

2 Why the United Kingdom?

1 In June 2000, 58 Chinese asylum hopefuls from the Fujian Province in southern China were found dead locked in a lorry's refrigerated sealed container, having been smuggled for months en route to Britain.

3 Procedures and process

1 Having an 'adversarial' judicial system means that in Britain the burden of proof that an applicant is not safe in his or her country of origin rests entirely upon the applicant. It is the Home Office's responsibility to oppose an applicant at every stage and not to alert him or her, or indeed the judge, to possible evidence that may help applicants to succeed.
2 Many refugees who were in the system for many years were accepted under the 1999 Immigration and Asylum process.
3 Home Office statistics.

4 Captives

1 Bail for Immigration Detainees and CCRJ's Bail Circle work together to provide sureties and legal representation for those incarcerated during the asylum process.
2 Home Office statistics show that people seeking asylum are still being locked up in prisons.
3 Leanne Webber and Loraine Gelsthorpe, *Deciding to Detain: How Decisions to Detain Asylum Seekers are Made at Ports of Entry*, Institute of Criminology, University of Cambridge, 2000.
4 Ibid.
5 By contrast, the annual figure for prisons is published.
6 Refugee Council, *Statistical Analysis* (January 1997).
7 C. K. Pourgourides, *A Second Exile: The Mental Health Implications of Detention of Asylum Seekers in the United Kingdom* (1996).
8 Home Office, White Paper, *Fairer, Faster and Firmer: Immigration and Asylum* (July 1998).
9 http://www.homeoffice.gov.uk/rds/pdfs2/asylumq302.pdf
Home Office statistics for the third quarter of 2002 stated that there were 115 asylum detainees in prisons.

5 Support

1 The Home Office said that non-statutory public local planning inquiries are to be held on the proposed centres at: Defence Storage and Distribution Centre (DSDC), Bicester, Oxfordshire, and RAF Newton, Nottinghamshire. Further work is required on the following three sites before a decision can be taken on whether to proceed to planning notifications: Sully Hospital, Cardiff; AirWest, Edinburgh; Hemswell Cliff, Lincolnshire. The Government announced in February 2003 that it was considering the suitability of a smaller-scale accommodation centre for asylum seekers at HMS Daedalus in Gosport, Hampshire. It has since

been announced that 'the centre planned for the Gosport site would be a smaller centre for single asylum seekers in an urban area'. The Home Office also confirmed (February 2003) that 'it will not be pursuing, for the trial, sites at Sully Hospital (South Glamorgan), AirWest (Edinburgh) and RAF Hemswell (Lincolnshire)'. It is, however, 'looking for sites in Scotland as an alternative to AirWest, Edinburgh'. See website at ch. 4, n. 9 above.

6 Integration

1 Sir William MacPherson, *The Stephen Lawrence Inquiry Report*, London: Home Office, February 1999.

7 Not just a refugee

1 The British Medical Association, *The Medical Profession and Human Rights: Handbook for a Changing Agenda* (July 2001); see also *Access to Health Care for Asylum Seekers* (January 2001).